LEABHARLANN CHONTAE LUIMNI
LIMERICK COUNTY LIBRARY

Historical Representation
and the Postcolonial Imaginary

Historical Representation and the Postcolonial Imaginary: Constructing Travellers and Aborigines

By

John Harnett

CAMBRIDGE SCHOLARS

PUBLISHING

Historical Representation and the Postcolonial Imaginary:
Constructing Travellers and Aborigines,
by John Harnett

This book first published 2011

Cambridge Scholars Publishing

12 Back Chapman Street, Newcastle upon Tyne, NE6 2XX, UK

British Library Cataloguing in Publication Data
A catalogue record for this book is available from the British Library

ISBN (10): 1-4438-2719-3, ISBN (13): 978-1-4438-2719-5

TABLE OF CONTENTS

ACKNOWLEDGEMENTS

A sincere thanks is extended to Paul Harrison and all of the other artists who so kindly contributed their images to the book. Also to Dr. Mícheál Ó hAodha, Department of History, University of Limerick – my thesis supervisor – for his support throughout the writing and publishing process. A sincere thank you is also extended to each of the organisations who provided us with permission to utilise their images under the Creative Commons image initiative.

For further information on Paul Harrison's work see:
http://www.c-s-p.org/flyers/Travellers--Friends1-4438-1257-9.htm and
http://www.rte.ie/tv/theafternoonshow/2009/1130/travellerfocusweekpaul harrison.html

CHAPTER ONE

INTRODUCTION:
ORAL HISTORY AND THE "OTHER"

1.1 Introduction

The quintessential revolution is that of the spirit, born of an intellectual
conviction of the need for change in those mental attitudes and values
which shape the course of a nation's development...
—Aung San Suu Kyi

Irish Travellers and Australian Aborigines are the indigenous peoples of
their respective countries. The histories of both groups have remained - for
the most part – unrecorded and what has been written has not been written
by members of either group. The pasts of these neglected social groups has
not changed. The history of both groups is constantly changing, however.

Oral history is a relatively new field in the realm of historiography. It
was not until the mid-twentieth century that its practice became
fashionable and more widely-researched. Oral history has the ability to
change the focus of traditional history; it can give voices to the voiceless,
bring down barriers and give life to communities (See Ritchie (1995,
2003), Shopes (2008), Perks and Thompson (1998, 2003). This continues
to be one of the great triumphs of oral history; its ability to give a voice
and therefore a history to communities and social groups who are
voiceless and occluded from historical representation. For socially
neglected groups, oral testimony creates the opportunity to recover the
past and in turn determine a present and a future. For the historian, the use
of oral testimony means that he or she must work closely with others. The
purpose of this project is concerned with the historian in his or her work
with the 'Other'.

The importance of oral history, particularly with regard to the 'Other',
or often-neglected groups in society, lies in the fact that a large percentage
of the world's population are non-literate, do not speak English and live in
abject poverty. In light of this, oral testimony is vital to the creation of
'Other' world histories. (See Chattopadhyaya and Gupta (1998), Kearney

(2002). The aforementioned social groups, Irish Travellers and Australian Aborigines, are examples of the 'Other', in both history and society. Theirs is a history often known only in the minds of their elders, stored and passed down through generations of storytelling and folklore. These two historically neglected social groups have strikingly common characteristics, both in terms of social standing and history. Oral history is the fundamental component by which both groups can construct their histories. The comparisons between both are many and thus certainly warrant a comparative study such as this, with oral history as the guiding light – that which propels both groups toward a better future. Oral history can help generate a more linear past, one which better suits the written form that defines the present-day. Both groups are indigenous and both were victims of colonisation at the hands of the British. Both have had to cope with decades, if not centuries, of stereotypes, negative media representation and poor government treatment. Both have suffered extremely low employment rates, and often as a corollary, high crime rates. According to statistics, both have relatively low life expectancy, due to poorer health and living conditions than settled people. In terms of history, representation has always been for them, rather than by them. Oral history has therefore given these groups the chance to create a cultural identity and a background.

Othering can be loosely defined as a way of depicting and characterising a race or community as intrinsically, (and often-negatively), different. In this 'difference', history has tended to be influenced by hierarchical and stereotypical thinking. Oral history has the potential to break these hierarchical barriers, by giving a voice to the Other, an Other which more often than not has hitherto been constructed in reified or negative prism. (See Broussard: 2003; Nkwi: 2010). The Other in the scope of this project, as mentioned, are the indigenous people of Ireland and Australia, Travellers and Aborigines. Both groups have been ostracised, remaining on the margins of society for the course of their pasts. Theirs is history as created by everyone but themselves. They are the Other, the 'Orient' that Edward Said spoke of in his seminal work *Orientalism*. They are the 'Orient' within the 'Occident'.[1] This project will endeavour to assess and compare the impact of oral history on the "Other".

This volume thus concentrates on the use of oral history in the empowerment of the above-mentioned groups. It begins by tracing the advent of oral history, before assessing its merits and potential drawbacks

---

[1] The Occident refers to Europe and the Western World. For Said, the Western World encompassed the Occident, while the East was the Orient.

more generally. Subsequently, the role of oral history regarding the Other will be discussed. Oral history is, and must be interdisciplinary. In light of this, I will explore the role of anthropology and ethnography in relation to the work of the oral historian. A large element in this project will be the focus on the history, or absence thereof- within the written and the visual spheres -of Irish Travellers and Australian Aborigines. The historical representations of both groups will be examined. Following this, the comparative nature of the histories of both groups will be assessed, in terms of aspects such as colonialism, media representations, and in particular, government attempts to 'fix' the groups.

1.2 Literature Review

For the purpose of this study it was essential to access sources on three key factors. Firstly, it was necessary to consult the main works in the field of oral history, and due to the interdisciplinary nature of the area, it was also necessary to delve into ethnography, sociology and postcolonialism amongst others. Secondly, an in depth study of sources involved with Irish Travellers was involved. The third faction in the search for sources was Australian Aborigines.

There is much and varied literature on and about oral history, testimony and tradition on the market in the present day. However, it is still difficult to look past Paul Thompson as the main practitioner of oral history. *The Voice of the Past*, although over thirty years old still remains one of the core texts in the field. For Thompson, the past is "handed down by oral tradition and written chronicle".[2] A combination of both is necessary for an eminent, whole history. Oral history gives history back to the people through their words. This is the theme of Thompson's teachings and technique. *The Voice of the Past* is vital therefore for both the theoretical perspectives it provides in relation to oral history but also use as regards its consideration of Otherness or the "Other". As Thompson states "it is social history, to which we now turn, that the relevance of oral evidence is most inescapable".[3]

An essential text for any study of oral history is Robert Perks and Alistair Thomson's compendium *The Oral History Reader*. It serves as a primary textbook and reference point for students, scholars and historians alike. Perks and Thomson bring together a collection of essays exploring every aspect of oral history, while offering their own commentary on each

---

[2] Paul Thompson, *The Voice of the Past.* (Oxford, 1978) p. 1.

[3] ibid, p. 86.

also. As is stated in the introduction to Part 1, Critical Perspectives, "The most distinctive contribution of oral history has been to include with the historical record the experiences and perspectives of groups of people who might otherwise have been hidden from history, perhaps written about by social observers or in official documents".[4] This statement encompasses the whole essence of this project, the neglected, the occluded, the hidden in history. As Perks and Thomson show in their collection, through oral history the working classes, cultural minorities and indigenous people have inscribed their experiences on the historical record and offered their own interpretations of their own history. *The Oral History Reader*, particularly in its second edition, covers all key aspects and debates that have raged in the oral history field, and the appearance of essays from eminent historians such as Paul Thompson, Alessandro Portelli, Michael Frisch, Linda Shopes and Katherine Borland, amongst others, serve to reinforce it as a primary text for oral history.

In addition, many more texts from the field were consulted for this study. Alessandro Portelli's *The Death of Luigi Trastulli and Other Stories* is a text which is also necessary to confer with in any study of oral history. Portelli is one of the foremost scholars on the interdisciplinary nature of oral history. His uses of the social and cultural facets of his fieldwork make for a more meaningful and rounded portrayal of what life was like for those studied. For Portelli it is not enough to merely give a voice to the voiceless, but also necessary to place these 'voiceless' in their relevant social and cultural surroundings at the time. Paula Hamilton and Linda Shopes are two of the leading women in the field, and their anthology *Oral History and Public Memories* is also a principal work on oral history and testimony. Published only last year, it contains up to date material from some of the leading experts of the practice. Other texts consulted under the sphere of oral history include Peter Burke's *History and the Historian in the Twentieth Century* and *New Perspectives on Historical Writing* John Tosh's *The Pursuit of History* and *Historians on History* and Ludmilla Jordonova's *History in Practice,* amongst many others. The main journal used to with regard to this project was *Oral History Review.*

As well as investigating the main scholars in the oral history field, it was also necessary to consult various texts regarding post-colonialism, ethnography and Othering. Frantz Fanon, although his work is over four decades old, is still a foremost and worthwhile, reference on post-colonial groups and Othering. His *The Wretched of the Earth* and *Black Skin, White Masks* are still regarded as powerful texts on colonisation and its

---

[4] Robert Perks and Alistair Thompson, *The Oral History Reader,* (London, 1998) p.9.

aftermath. From his works, it is possible to view where much of experts in the area have taken their theories and ideas from. For an understanding of ethnography and particularly ethnocentrism it was essential to consult some textbooks in the area. Martyn Hammersley and Paul Atkinson's *Ethnography: Principles in Practice, Third Editon* (2007), was the most up to date work consulted. It gave a basic overview of ethnography, without getting involved with the notion of post-colonialism and the Other. John and Jean Comaroff's *Ethography and the Historical Imagination* did in fact deal with ethnocentrism and postcolonialism in history, as the title may suggest. Other works conferred with included Norman K. Denzin's *Interpretive Ethnography*. Regarding post-colonial thought itself, a useful publication proved to be Iain Chambers and Lidia Curti's *The Post-Colonial Question*.

Primary material used as the basis of the study included various reports, articles and publications on Irish Travellers and Australian Aborigines. Concerning Travellers, *The Irish Folklore Commission 1952 Tinker Questionnaire,* the *1963 Report of the Commission on Itinerancy* and the *1995 Report of the Task Force on the Travelling Community*, as well as the *Executive Summary* of the report were the main documents used. Regarding Aborigines, the most comprehensive, and landmark report produced in their history, the 1997 *Bringing Them Home: National Inquiry into the Separation of Aboriginal and Torres Strait Islander Children from Their Families* was used. Other excellent sources include Aboriginal testimony in Bain Attwood and Fiona Magowan's *Telling Stories: Indigenous History and Memory in Australia and New Zealand* and letter transcripts in Henry Reynolds *Dispossession: Black Australians and White Invaders.*

As the majority of this study concerned the historical representations of Irish Travellers and Australian Aborigines, it was necessary to consult the leading historians in both fields. Regarding Irish Travellers, Míchael Ó hAodha's *Irish Travellers: Representations and Realities* is one of the most up to date works, which pays particular attention to Othering and representations in the history of the community, which are key aspects of this study. Other major works consulted with regard to the history of the Irish Travelling community, or least representations of that history, include Jane Helleiner's *Irish Travellers: Racism and the Politics of Culture,* and Aoife Bhreatnach's *Becoming Conspicuous: Irish Travellers, Society and State 1922-1970.* Both works are quite comprehensive in terms of twentieth century representation and legislation regarding Travellers. Hellenier's publication provides an excellent viewpoint into the history and society of the Irish Travelling community. Firstly, she is

Canadian, and thus removed from inherent Irish stereotypes and negativity towards the community, and secondly, she spent nine months living amongst Travellers in Galway in the mid 1980s as part of her ethnographic research. Therefore, she worked closely with the community itself, a point which is central to this study. It synthesises history, politics and ethnography, unlike many other works in the field. Helleiner's work is vital in any study of Irish Travellers. Aoife Bhreatnach's *Being Conspicuous* is also an excellent work regarding Travellers. It concentrates on history and politics concerning Travellers, tracing the circumstances that caused their marginalisation, examining government attempts to 'fix' them, and the implications of both during the twentieth century. *Travellers: Citizens of Ireland*, edited by Erica Sheehan, was another major work used. The importance of this publication lies in the fact that it is made up of testimony from the Travelling community itself. The book, then, is representative of this study, as its attempts to allow Travellers both to be represented historically, and to represent themselves. Other publications consulted included the influential but dated works of the Gmelch's, George and Sharon, namely George Gmelch's *The Irish Tinkers: The Urbanisation of an Itinerant People* and Sharon Gmelch's *Tinkers and Travellers: Ireland's Nomads*. Míchael Ó hAodha's collections *Migrants and Memory: The Forgotten Postcolonials* and *On the Margins of Memory: Recovering the Migrant Voice* were also particularly helpful regarding postcolonialism and Traveller representations. Other sources consulted in reference to this section of the study included journals such as *Anthropological Quarterly* and *Sociology*, and web resources such as *The Patrin Web Journal* and *Pavee Point* home page.

The major works consulted as part of researching the Aboriginal community were, as one would anticipate, from Australian authors. Stuart Macintyre is one of the country's leading academic historian, and a central figure in the 'History Wars' which Australian historians have been embroiled in, in recent years. His works *A Concise History of Australia* and *The History Wars* provided particularly detailed, though sometimes ambivalent constructs of the subject matter. Though the term concise may be seen as curtailing the detailed history of the country in a brief manner, Macintyre certainly does not. *The History Wars* is particularly helpful regarding the politicisation of Australian history, which is documented well by the author. Bain Attwood is another member in the top echelons of Australian academic history. His *Telling the Truth about Aboriginal History* is vital to a study of that same history mentioned in the title. His work is largely aimed at discrediting the main critic of the 'true' Aboriginal history, Keith Windschuttle, whose own book, *The Fabrication of Australian History* attempts aims to discredit Aboriginal claims of atrocities and genocide at the hands of British colonisers. In this manner, Attwood's publication is imperative in attempts to construct an Aboriginal history, and studies in the representation of such. Another work of Attwood's, which he edited with Fiona MacGowan, also proved beneficial. *Telling Stories: Indigenous History and Memory in Australia and New Zealand* brings together a collection of essays on indigenous history and oral testimony. The book included excellent primary material in the form of this oral testimony of Aboriginal victims of the Stolen Generations. Henry Reynolds is another historian who has gained minor celebrity status in Australia due to the nature of the 'History Wars', which has been played out in the general Australian media. Reynolds collaboration with Aborigines led to ground-breaking events in Aboriginal history, such as the granting of land rights to Aborigine Eddie Mabo in 1992. Reynolds' *Dispossession: Black Australians and White Invaders* provided tremendous source material in the form of many letter transcripts from the nineteenth century. Reynolds' authority as one of the foremost and eminent Australian historians makes his *Dispossession* and *Frontier: Reports from the Edge of White Settlement* key texts in the area. Ann McGrath's edited collection, *Contested Ground: Australian Aborigines under the British Crown* was useful regarding colonisation. Malcolm Prentis' *A Study in Black and White: The Aborigines in Australian* History was helpful regarding background material but was outdated, having been published in 1975. Other helpful publications included Geoffrey Partington's *The Australian History of Henry Reynolds* and Michael Meadows' *Voices in the Wilderness: Images of Aboriginal People in the Australian Media*. Web sources used in the area included transcripts of speeches by former Australian Prime Minister, Paul Keating, found at the *Online Opinion* web site. Online reports from leading Australian newspaper *The Australian* also provided excellent insight.

CHAPTER TWO

ORAL HISTORY AND THE OCCLUDED PEOPLES

E.H. Carr asked "What is history?" What was his answer? Is history the past, or is it the study of the past? If so, is historiography the study of history? If both these are true, where does oral history fit? Is it a practice in its own right; is it a facet of 'history', or a mode of historiography? John Tosh simply defines it as "what actually happened in the past and the representation of that past in the work of historians"[1]. Ludmilla Jordanova defines history as having,

> a number of meanings, and a wide range of connotations, some of which are charged   with intense emotion. We use it invoke the authority of precedents, to refer to what is no longer relevant, to endow objects with value and status, and to mobilise longings for a better world.[2]

The last part of Jordanova's description states "to mobilise longings for a better world". If this is accurate, has history in the last century or so, mobilised these "longings"? Perhaps it has, but for the most part, it has 'mobilised' them from the perspective of the winners, from the top-down. Where is the history of the losers? Where are the histories from 'below'? They are in the process of being told, documented and stored in the annals of history, but this is only a very recent phenomenon. The following chapter will concentrate on oral history, its history, development, uses and especially its ability to bring the 'losers', the 'below' and the 'Other' into historical scribe.

---

[1] John Tosh, *The Pursuit of History (4th Ed.)* (Harlow, 2006) xvix.
[2] Ludmilla Jordanova, *History in Practice (2nd Ed.)* (New York, 2006) p. 13.

2.1 The Early History and Development of Oral History

"Tete ke asom ene Kayere"[3]

So the above Ghanaian proverb translates, "Ancient things remain in the ear". It was not until the nineteenth century that history became academic. Before this, all history had to rely on oral testimony. The past was passed from generation to generation through word of mouth. Perks and Thomson assert that oral evidence has been used since ancient times, where history relied on eye-witness accounts of significant events. Donald P. Ritchie travels as far back as the Spanish conquests of the Americas in his *Doing Oral History;* "the Spanish chroniclers relied on oral sources to reconstruct the history of the indigenous people, from the Aztecs to the Incas".[4] It was in the nineteenth century that the development of an academic history discipline led to a primacy of archival research and documentary sources, and a marginalisation of oral evidence.[5] Oral history became initially popular as a practice in the 1960s, a time when many marginalised groups were seeking to be heard. The 1960s played host to the Feminist movement and the Civil Right movement, to name but two, movements which oral history was utterly representative of, and partly responsible for the empowerment of. Therefore, while oral history and testimony have been practiced since ancient times, oral history itself as a practice is relatively in its infancy, only becoming popular in the mid-twentieth century, arguably in the aftermath of World War II, with oral history became vital in the testimonies of Holocaust victims.

Oral history thus only became academic in the twentieth century. As Rebecca Sharpless states in "The History of Oral History", "In the twentieth century, the methodology rose from several directions"[6]. Methodology had never been a term used in relation to oral history, and perhaps is still not accepted by some traditional historians. Oral history arguably was not accepted as a necessary practice by many until much later, and conceivably is still not. Many traditional historians, who advocate a 'top-down', elitist history, have never accepted the need for oral testimony, particularly of marginalised, hidden groups. Sharpless states that it was in the 1940s that oral history became unified in the Western academic world, particularly in the post-war era. One of the first

---

[3] Rebecca Sharpless, "The History of Oral History", in Charlton et al, *Handbook of Oral History,* (Plymouth,2006) p.19.
[4] Donald P. Ritchie, *Doing Oral History (2nd ed.)* (New York, 2006).
[5] Perks and Thomson, p.1.
[6] Sharpless, p.19.

institutionalised oral history projects was created by Allan Nevins at Columbia University in 1948.[7] Nevin's project was designed to "collect the reminiscences of major figures in contemporary public life, and it served as kind of an oral appendix to the published memoirs of many of these people".[8] However, Nevins' advocacy of oral history, but also his efforts to encourage historians to aim for a more popular audience were greeted with scepticism at the time by many professional historians. His criticism of what he described as "dry-as-dust" academics alienated some of them.[9] Also in 1948, the first American-made tape recordings were recorded. The first Oral History Office opened in 1954 at the University of California.[10] It is widely recognised that the oral history 'boom' took place in the 1960s, when research in the practice expanded dramatically. The availability of portable cassette recorders, invented by Philips in 1963, had much to do with this.[11] Ritchie goes back somewhat further, stating that the Works Progress Administration's hiring of unemployed writers to chronicle the lives of ordinary people during the Depression in the 1930s, was perhaps closer to the advent of oral history as a practice.[12] More so to do with this 'boom' though was the increase of socialist and minority movements of the age. The Feminist movement, the Civil Rights movement, the Vietnam War and the various student "revolts" of the late 1960s all involved activist activities on the part of ordinary people, not kings or great leaders or statesmen. As Hamilton and Shopes attest "Oral history emerged as a widespread practice in relation to the democratising of history in the 1960s, fuelled by decolonisation and the feminist and civil rights movements".[13] Oral history documented the lives of these 'ordinary' people, in the way traditional, elitist history never had, or would. As stated previously, it gave that 'voice' to the voiceless and in doing this historians of the field hoped they could foster social change. Jordanova states that the term 'academic discipline' implies elaborate institutional, professional and communications structures.[14] By the end of the 1960s, oral history

---

[7] Ibid, p.22.

[8] Mark Feldstein, "Kissing Cousins: Journalism and Oral History", in *Oral History Review,* Spring 2004.

[9] Jerrold Hirsh, "Before Columbia: The FWP and American Oral History Research", in *Oral History Review*, Summer 2007, p.8.

[10] Sharpless, p.23.

[11] Ibid, p.23.

[12] Ritchie, p.21.

[13] Paula Hamilton and Linda Shopes, *Oral History and Public Memories,* (Philadelphia, 2008) p.9.

[14] Jordanova, p.59.

certainly had become an academic discipline in its own right. The practice continued to grow, and in 1968, the Oral History Association drew up a code of Ethics for interviewers. These maintained that the interviews "wishes must govern the conduct of an interview".[15] The growing importance of these various social and ethnic groups which arose in the late 1960s and early 1970s fuelled the subsequent interest in documenting their histories. The challenge for oral historians to overcome at the onset of the movement as a practice was the defence of the reliability and validity of interviews,[16] the reliability being the consistency with which the interviewees tell their story, and the validity being the agreement between the interview itself and other sources in a historical context. In 1971, the Oral History Society of England published its first journal and in January 1973, the Oral History Review, one of the foremost oral history publications in the present day, released its first publication.[17] As the century wore on, more and more oral history societies were born, and many more journals have been set up. Oral history is therefore very much an academic practice in its own right in the present day. In later years, the focus of oral history and memory studies have shifted from the empowerment of the individual to that of societies at large, groups of individuals testimonies, rather than the singular. As Sharpless states, "the internet changes everything, but the basic dynamic of two people sitting and talking about the past has remained largely unchanged".[18]

2.2 The Use and Benefits of Oral History

"Every old man that dies is a library that burns".[19]

Oral history is dependent on this "old man". It is dependent on the person who is interviewing this old man, and it is dependent on the relationship between these two. This is essence of oral history; the ability to retrieve seemingly forgotten information from oral testimonies and creating a historical fit and social construct, to use the information garnered to create history. As Paul Thompson, arguably the chief authority in the field, states "Past is handed down by oral tradition and written chronicle",[20] meaning testimony and documentation is necessary for an empirical history. Oral

---

[15] Sharpless, p.27.
[16] Ibid, p.30.
[17] Ibid, p.32.
[18] Ibid, p.38.
[19] Perks and Thomson, viii.
[20] Thompson, p.1.

history is often more precise than traditional, establishment history. Most accounts of the past are through the spoken word, and so historians must use oral techniques to document events which have not been recorded in history. So to define oral history, again using the words of Paul Thompson, one could perhaps call it "the interviewing of eye-witness participants in the events of the past for the purposes of historical reconstruction".[21] Thompson defended oral history against its critics, those who claimed it to be an unreliable historical source, and was determined to prove its legitimacy. In terms of the reverence afforded to his work today, he certainly succeeded in this regard.

Oral history makes for a history which is not just richer, more vivid and heart-rending, but truer.[22] Oral history functions to allow the story of "what really happened" to be told. Traditional, and so-called establishment history, portrayed, and perhaps still does, a 'top-down' history of 'great men', kings, political leaders and people in positions of power. Oral history allows "heroes not just from the leaders, but from the unknown majority of the people".[23] It is the people's history. It offers a radical transformation of the social meaning of history. Oral history offers a form of cultural and national identity for the masses. Essentially it offers a route into history to those who have been 'hidden', deprived in the historical wilderness for the course of their pasts. This provides the platform for this study, a study of oral history in the empowerment of groups who have been hidden and neglected by history.

2.3 Oral History and the Creation of Histories of Neglected Groups

"Oral history gives history back to the people in their own words. And in giving a past it also helps them towards a future of their own making".[24]

As previously stated, in the modern age, oral history has played, and must continue to play, a vital, intrinsic role in history and historiography. The study of history has been changing constantly over the last fifty or so years. As the study of history changes, so then does history itself, in a sense. Traditional history is a history of the 'winners', a 'top-down' history. Conventional modern day history must be much more than that. It must be a multi-faceted study of the past, including sociology, geography,

---

[21] Perks and Thomson, p.9.
[22] Thompson, p.99.
[23] Ibid, p.21.
[24] Ibid, p.1.

politics, anthropology and economics, amongst others. As society has
progressed in the modern era, so has history. Histories of the 'other' have
become more and more mainstream towards the end of the twentieth, and
start of the twenty-first centuries. To conduct a study of the 'other' in
history, oral testimony is the historian's most indispensable tool.
Therefore, oral history has provided historians, in recent years, the ability
oral history working classes, cultural minorities and indigenous peoples, to
attempt to establish studies of otherwise neglected social groupings.
Through amongst others, have "inscribed their experiences on the
historical record, and offered their own interpretations of history".[25] To
create a history of any neglected group is generally to create a 'history
from below'. Jim Sharpe, in his essay "History from Below", describes it
as "an exploration of the historical experiences of those men and women
whose existence is often ignored, taken for granted or mentioned in
passing in mainstream history".[26] It can both restore history to groups who
thought they had lost it, or to groups who never had it all.

Perks and Thomson, in their introduction to the "Critical Developments"
section of *The Oral History Reader*, state,

> The most distinctive contribution of oral history has been to include within
> the historical record the experiences and perspectives of groups of people
> who might otherwise have been hidden from history, perhaps written
> about by social observers in official documents.[27]

This statement engenders the entire essence of 'history from below', and
the empowerment of neglected social groups in history. The groups
concentrated on for this study, Irish Travellers and Australian Aborigines,
represent those "hidden from history", those for whom oral testimony has
been, and is, necessary to document their lives and pasts. Paul Thompson
even names Aboriginals as an example of such in *The Voice of the Past,*
particularly in relation to colonialism,

> Other minorities are the survivors of conquest, or traditional social
> outcasts. American Indians, Australian Aborigines and gypsies of Europe
> are all persecuted minorities, misleadingly documented by a hostile
> majority, but preserving their strong oral traditions, to which a more
> understanding approach to their past becomes possible.[28]

---

[25] Perks and Thompson, p.9.
[26] Jim Sharpe, "History from Below", in Peter Burke (ed.), *New Perspectives on
Historical Writing (2nd Ed.),* (Oxford, 2001) p.26.
[27] Perks and Thomson, p.9.
[28] Thompson, p.97.

The "hostile majority" here represents those who have attempted to write histories of those same neglected groups, members of the media industry and often the general, settled, population itself. History in this way brings the social classes together; it joins the Aborigine and Traveller with the historian, enabling their pasts to be documented in a way that it most likely never has before, i.e. positively. Traditional history was, as the main practitioners of oral history will assert, concentrated on, and was made up of, "reigns and dynasties".[29] Reigns and dynasties mean very little, if anything, to neglected social groups, or ethnically rejected groups. In this regard, oral historians have addressed this gaping hole in history. What is world history, if not just that, a history of the world? Traditional history generally documented a history of the 'first world'. This is not an empirical world history. This is establishment, 'top-down' history. Donald Ritchie states that history is the verdict of "those who weren't there on those who were".[30] Whether Aborigines or Travellers were "there" or not is generally irrelevant in history, because the groups have either been unable to record it due to high illiteracy levels, or simply had no interest in it, again due to low levels of education. It is arguably the duty then of the oral and social historian to document a history of groups such as these, history which is necessary for their empowerment and future. Most traditional historical work that has been carried out on neglected groups has usually been without any involvement from any member of said groups, and if there has been involvement it often has been recorded negatively. The "History Wars" in Australia are an example. Social historians have argued on the side of Aborigines regarding the atrocities of the past, whereas, for the most part, traditional historians have argued that there is no evidence that such atrocities happened. John Tosh argues that oral history is "the raw material of social memory"[31]. This is a prime example of the need and use of oral testimony. While the Aboriginal people may not have literal, linear documentation of the past, work with oral and social historians regarding memory has enabled their story to at least be heard. Similarly, Travellers have had to wait until the later decades of the twentieth century to begin to have their story told and recorded. This will be concentrated on further in later chapters.

---

[29] Ibid, p.2
[30] Donald P. Ritchie, *Doing Oral History,* (New York, 1995) p. 8
[31] Tosh, p.323

2.4 Ethnocentrism and the Other

Why have traditional historians chosen not to focus on groups of lower social standing in their work since history became academic? The straightforward answer would be that it is simply easier to document a history of the victors. Where oral history is not overly necessary, where the result, in history, is plain for all to see, the historians position is extremely tenable. However, is that historian doing his/her job by ignoring the 'losers'?

Ethnography can be defined as a descriptive account of a community or culture, usually one located outside the West.[32] Ethnocentrism then can be defined as the inclination to view one's own culture as better than others, by viewing the others as strange and different. Ethnographic scholars Ross Hammond and Robert Axelrod, in "The Evolution of Ethnocentrism", characterize it as

> a nearly universal syndrome of attitudes and behaviours, typically including in-group favouritism. Empirical evidence suggests that a predisposition to favour in groups can be easily triggered by even arbitrary group distinctions and that preferential cooperation within groups occurs even when it is individually costly.[33]

Ethnocentrism is central to the study of Aboriginal and Traveller people, as it is the fundamental principle of Othering in history. Othering lies at the very heart of this study. Any study of neglected social groups in history encompasses a study of the 'Other'. Travellers are the 'Other', and 'Aborigines' are the 'Other'. Said's *Orientalism,* as mentioned previously, displays how the 'Orient' was 'Othered' by Western society because they wanted to control it. Similarly, Aborigines and Travellers have been 'Othered' in history, because they were misunderstood, mistreated and generally unwanted. Othering constitutes almost the dehumanisation of social groups. This Othering then creates a distrust and separateness, which is clearly evident in the case studies used here. The divide between the indigenous and settled populations of both Australia and Ireland is still extremely wide. Oral history has been the 'carrot' which has enabled less of the 'stick' approach in recent years, as settled society begins to learn more about the indigenous 'Other'.

---

[32] Paul Atkinson and Martin Hammersley, *Ethnography: Principles in Practice (3rd Ed.)* (New York, 2007), p.1.
[33] Ross A. Hammond and Robert Axelrod, "The Evolution of Ethnocentrism", in *Journal of Conflict Resolution, Vol.50.* (2006) p.926.

Inherent in many cases of Othering in society is post-colonialism. In the case of both Australian Aborigines and Irish Travellers, this is inextricably the case. This is another of the close comparisons between the groups; they are both indigenous groups of post-colonial nations, conquered by the British, and still in search of identity and acceptance in their own countries. In this regard, both groups were marginalised within imperial discourse. Post-colonialism has witnessed the break-up of empires, decolonisation, the formation of new states and power blocs and the destruction of old nations. Catherine Hall asserts that such shifts have, in many ways, had a destabilising effect on the world, creating contradictory tendencies- globalism alongside localism, new nationalisms and ethnic identities alongside the international communication highways.[34] In light of this, it is the function of oral historians and associated ethnographers to rescue "localism" and the "ethnic identities" that are inherent there. Globalism and globalisation do not account for the documentation of histories and empowerment of neglected social groups. Oral history certainly does. Therefore, oral history is intrinsic to the past and present of post-colonial nations, social groups and indigenous and cultural 'others'. Othering can thus be described, in terms of historical approach, as a means of comparing oneself but at the same time distancing oneself from others, in this case, the Other. As is evident in the works of Said, Frantz Fanon and Homi Bhabha, amongst others, post-colonialism is central to the creation of this Other. 'Otherness', for Fanon, is the search for identity, the quest for meaning for the "wretched of the Earth".[35] In these terms, the groups used in the scope of this study most certainly embody "the wretched of the earth". Fanon asserts that the central idea of colonialism is "that the confrontation of 'civilised' and 'primitive' men creates a special situation- and brings about the emergence of a mass of illusions and misunderstandings that only a psychological analysis can place and define".[36] If Fanon is correct, and this is true, then this psychological analysis is necessary for the empowerment of post-colonial peoples both mentally and physically. The fact that it very rarely, if ever, happened means that the "mass of illusions and misunderstandings" inherent in neglected post-colonial groups is still present in the modern

---

[34] Catherine Hall, "Histories, Empires and the Post-Colonial Moment", in Iain Chambers and Lidia Curti, *The Post-Colonial Question: Common Skies, Divided Horizons* (London, 1996) p.65

[35] *The Wretched of the Earth* is the title of Fanon's 1963 work, called "the greatest masterpiece of anti-colonial struggle" by John-Paul Sartre

[36] Frantz Fanon, *Black Skin, White Masks* (London, 1986) p. 85

day, a fact which is entrenched in the situations of both Australian Aborigines and Irish Travellers.

Oral history endeavours to provide a platform for historically neglected, post-colonial groups, such as Australian Aborigines and Irish Travellers, to overcome these very real and very obvious barriers, a platform for which to create a past and envision a future. However, can history ever really be objective? Despite the historian's best attempts, it is impossible to rid oneself entirely of the ethnocentrism that dogs our desire to know others.[37] The problem for the historian then is representation. Oral history must, by its very nature, be interdisciplinary. History itself is eclectic, hence the range of its debts and the complexity of its relations with other disciplines.[38] Therein lies an ethnographic problem. Representation "involves the assumption that much, if not all, qualitative and ethnographic writing is a narrative production, structured by a logic that separates writer, text and subject matter".[39] The historian must validate what he/she has been told, which becomes problematic when a linear, documented history is not available. The historian must, for that reason, take as many of these "narratives" as possible to try to discern historical fact. The historian, when dealing with the Other, must be historian, socialist, anthropologist and ethnographer, amongst many other. They must "cast the bourgeois subject out of the anthropological fold".[40] Representation is the primary focus of the oral historian in this regard, and he/she must be multi-faceted and interdisciplinary to do so. The history of neglected social and post-colonial groupings - (See Bhreatnach: 2006; Court: 1985; Lanters: 2009) must be considered through the same prism also. The following chapter will provide an overview of the history and historiography, of two such groups i.e. the Irish Travellers and the Australian Aborigines.

---

[37] John and Jean Comaroff, *Ethnography and the Historical Imagination* (Oxford, 1992) p. 10

[38] Jordanova, p.80

[39] Norman K. Denzin, *Interpretive Ethnography: Ethnographic Practices in the 21st Century* (London, 1997) p.4

[40] Comaroff, p.10

CHAPTER THREE

HISTORY AS QUEST:
THE CASE OF IRISH TRAVELLERS
AND AUSTRALIAN ABORIGINES

3.1 The Quest for History: Travellers and Aborigines and 'History from Below'

History may not be a subject of major interest to many members of the Travelling community. In the same way that Aboriginal history is not written, for the most part, by Aborigines, and a history of an African tribe is most likely not going to be written by a member of that tribe, the history of Irish Travellers is not written by Travellers. There are several reasons for this. The seeming disinterest of the Travelling community in education leaves many non or semi-literate, and incapable of writing any kind of history. Stereotypes play an intrinsic role in Irish society, and while this is not indicative of all Travellers, the self-same stereotypes remain. Much of the general public may not have any interest in history, but perhaps it is easy to have no interest in a history when one already has one. For Travellers, this is not such a ready commodity. History is important in understanding the present, as well as the past, and this may be where the root of at least some of the anti-Traveller prejudices in modern Ireland lie. A history of Travellers engenders a history of the 'Other', and most certainly a history from below. Oral history is vital in the creation of a Traveller history. Private testimonies represent, predominantly, the only method historians can possibly have in seeking to explain the Traveller past. It is ultimately the only way, due to the high levels of non-literacy among the community, and therefore, the lack of any written history or records. There are huge similarities here inherent in Australia's History Wars. Aboriginal history is utterly comparable in its status of 'history from below', and its utter dependence on oral testimony. The difficulties in the quest for Aboriginal history have resulted in the History Wars. Historians have argued fervently over the actual extent of the atrocities committed against the Aboriginal race in history, causing these 'Wars'. This is the dilemma of having no recorded history. It is primarily the settled community who have attempted to resolve the problem of the lack of Traveller history. There are, of course, massively diverse opinions of Travellers within the settled community, and then, obviously between historians. In the same way as Aborigines do not write their histories, neither do Travellers, therein creating the problem of diversity of opinions. Any given aspect of Traveller history, or Traveller life for that matter, may, and most likely does, differ between Traveller and historian, leading to another potential 'History War'. The comparisons between the lifestyles and histories, or perhaps pasts rather than histories, of these groups are many, and make a comparative study in terms of this lifestyle and history a very viable and interesting study.

A problem recurrent in the history of 'Othering' is ethnocentrism. This is the tendency to look upon a certain culture as logical or sensible, while viewing others as somewhat bizarre, strange or even dangerous. This problem is largely recurrent due to the fact that histories of the said groups have very rarely been carried out by members of those groups; they are created by members of what one would term as western society. Oral history, then, is essential in the creation of history of the 'other', and in the empowerment of neglected social groups. The main problem in this regard lies in interpretation. As Trevor Lummins attests in his essay on "Structure and Validity in Oral Evidence", "the problem at the heart of using the interview method in history still remains that of moving from the individual account to a social interpretation".[1] The problem the historian remains- is the individual experience being accounted entirely reliable, as does the problem for the 'neglected social group'- is the historians interpretation going to be contextualized in a manner which is agreeable to the interviewee. Lummins asserts that while retrospective interviewing and oral testimony is necessary, and capable of establishing factual data, it must be interpreted and structured in terms of other gathered data.[2] If this process is carried out correctly, and is as objective as possible, then it is absolutely vital, and utterly invaluable to the documentation and empowerment of 'other' groups. In the case of the Australian Aborigine and the Irish Traveller, often the "individual account" is almost vilified, discredited. The historian must ensure this does not happen with the facts he/she has been given. Katherine Borland speaks of the need for a

---

[1] Trevor Lummins, "Structure and Validity in Oral Evidence", in Robert Perks and Alistair Thomson (eds.), *The Oral History Reader* (New York, 2006) p. 255.
[2] Ibid, p. 255.

"negotiative interpretative process"[3] in her essay "That's Not What I Said". She explains for herself, as a folklorist, the need for a skilfully told story, but invariably the need for the self same tale to be contextualized properly. She explains this as the difference between "the thinking subject and the narrated event and thinking subject and the narrative event".[4] In this way, oral testimony must be structured and contextualized correctly, but must retain objectivity, as far as possible, on the part of the historian.

3.2 The history of Irish Travellers

Interest in the history of Travellers was peripheral for much of the nineteenth and early twentieth century's.[5] The Gypsy Lore Society, set up in Britain in 1888, began to stimulate an interest in the culture of the 'Other', gypsies, nomads, travellers. It was set up by members of the urban middle class, who were fascinated by groups who appeared to be "unblemished by the ravages and corruption of modernity"[6]. It would be very difficult to affirm if the same were true now. Therefore, from the outset, the history of Travellers was studied and written by non-Travellers. W.B. Yeats was said to be a member of the Gypsy Lore Society. Míchael Ó hAodha asserts that this interest in gypsy and Traveller culture subsided for the first half of the 20th century. A major catalyst which thrust Irish Travellers back into the construct of Irish history was the "Report of the Commission on Itinerancy", a government report, released in 1963[7]. The report was, by all means, incredibly short-sighted. It proposed the assimilation of the Travelling community, without envisaging any major problems. The report was in no way an anthropological or historically merited paper, as it had little or no input from either field. Diarmuid Ferriter states that the 1963 report "suggested that the real solution lay in coaxing the Travellers into becoming settled"[8]. It was compiled by non-Travellers, with very little actual study into the lives and culture of the community. While ethnicity was not the political 'buzz word' in 1963 that

---

[3] Katherine Borland, "'That's not what I said' Interpretative Conflict in Oral Narrative Research", in Robert Perks and Alistair Thomson (eds.), *The Oral History Reader* (New York, 2006) p. 310.

[4] Ibid, p. 311.

[5] Míchael Ó hAodha, *Irish Travellers: Representations and Realities* (Dublin, 2006) p.13.

[6] Ibid, p. 15.

[7] Ibid, p. 35.

[8] Diarmuid Ferriter, *The Transformation of Ireland 1900-2000* (London, 2004) p.594.

it is now, the government cleverly avoided mentioned anything even marginally related to the ethnic status of Travellers. In hindsight, the report arguably served to help Travellers develop their 'ethnicity theory', which the likes of Martin Collins and members of Pavee Point, and the Irish Traveller Movement constantly refer to in the media. While the community are often silent in response to constant, and often sensationalist, media criticisms of them, the Travellers who do speak publicly on issues that affect their community usually belong to these groups[9]. The aforementioned assimilatory and conciliatory methods have, in terms of modern Irish society at least, served only to widen the divide between the settled and Travelling community's. Now more than ever, Travellers are a separate entity, and perhaps, ethnic group.

Traveller woman, Mrs. Ward pictured outside her trailer (caravan) in Tullamore, County Offaly. (*P. Harrison Collection*).

---

[9] Eamon Dillon, *The Outsiders: Exposing the Secretive World of Ireland's Travellers* (Dublin 2006) p.11.

Group of Irish Travellers photographed outside their site in County Kilkenny, Ireland. (*P. Harrison Collection*).

Where and when, then, did Travellers come from? The aforementioned lack of documented history of the group means there is no definitive answer, and attempts at answering have only become apparent in historical constructs in the last few decades. A group's history is nearly always predicated on historical origins that can be identified and located.[10] This is the problem endemic in the history of a marginalised group. Michael McDonagh, part of the new breed of Travellers speaking for, and about Travellers, asserts in Erica Sheehan's *Travellers: Citizens of Ireland*, that there are many theories about the origin of the Travelling people. The most common one, he states, which has had most support from the settled community is that Irish Travellers are the descendants of the people who lost their land at the time of the Famine.[11] This is though, arguably, at odds with the Traveller mantra of nomadism as a way of life. To support this

---

[10] Ó hAodha, p.1.
[11] Michael McDonagh, "Origins of the Travelling People", in Erica Sheehan (ed.), *Travellers: Citizens of Ireland* (Dublin, 2000) p.22.

theory would associate Travellers as "failed settled people"[12], and would actually make subsequent government attempts at assimilation and settlement, attempts at re-assimilation and re-settlement, which quite clearly was, as Helleiner contends, the justification of the state settlement policy in the 1960s.[13] For the Travelling community, this certainly would not be the way in which they view their history, especially as indigenous people. As Míchael Ó hAodha states, "Irish Travellers are an indigenous minority who have traditionally lived on the margins of mainstream Irish society".[14] If this is true, how then can Travellers have descended from those who lost their lands during the Famine, when those, mostly farmers and labourers, made up a large portion of this mainstream Irish society at the time?

The origin of the Traveller people is therefore either unknown or very varied. The Famine theory may have some basis, but for Travellers is certainly not how they see themselves as having originated. Leading Traveller activist, and author of several books including leading autobiography *My Life on the Road*, Nan Joyce states,

Some of my ancestors went on the road in the Famine but more of them have been travelling for hundreds of years- we're not drop-outs like some people think. The Travellers have been in Ireland since St. Patrick's time, there's a lot of history behind them though there's not much written down- it's what you get from your grandfather and what he got from his grandfather.[15]

---

[12] Ibid, p.22.

[13] Jane Helleiner, *Irish Travellers: Racism and the Politics of Culture* (Toronto, 2000) p.30.

[14] Ó hAodha, p.9.

[15] Helleiner, p.29.

Irish Traveller "Smurf" Riley pictured with his daughter, Jessica, County Tipperary, Ireland. (*P. Harrison Collection*).

This statement encompasses the very essence of oral history in the empowerment of historically neglected groups; i.e. the scope of this project. The history that we are familiar with regarding Travellers is that which has been handed down, and historically constructed by oral historians. Travellers have been constructed as an indigenous minority.[16] Considering, there are only around 35,000 Travellers living in the Republic of Ireland, and a further 6000-7000 in Northern Ireland[17], they are certainly a minority. Ó hAodha asserts that the earliest Irish oral history refers to "fir siúil" and "mná siúil", walking or travelling men and women. Some of these were bards and musicians, others were tradesmen, fairground people and labourers. Others were beggars. These people were

---

[16] Ibid, p.29.
[17] Hayes, p.9.

"the antecedents of the group known until recently in Ireland as "tinkers",
now called Travellers".[18] These people were nomadic all year round,
which is what set them apart from settled people. However, in saying this,
there is no definitive answer as to the origins of Travellers in history. This
brings the question of cultural legitimacy into question; if they have no
documented history, how can they lay claim to indigenous and ethnic
rights. Cultural legitimacy is also a problem for the Aboriginal people
which will be discussed later. As mentioned, Travellers are thought to
have descended from peasants who lost their lands during the Famine.
There is also a school of thought which claims that they were "native
chiefs dispossessed by English colonial policies during colonisation".[19]
This is another key area where Traveller and Aboriginal history is
comparable; both being the indigenous peoples of their respective
countries at the advent of colonisation at British hands.

Well-known Irish Traveller balladeer and musician Patrick "Pecker" Dunne. (*P. Harrison Collection*).

---

[18] Ibid, p.10.
[19] Ibid, p. 11.

Whatever the definitive origin of the Travelling people, it was in the nineteenth century, as mentioned, that they became the subject of historical, social and anthropological study. It was only with the foundation of the Gypsy Lore Society, in Britain in 1888, that the cultures of communities such as Travellers came into question. In light of this, documented Traveller history, at least to some extent, can be traced back to around this time. Regarding the notion of Travellers a having descended from Famine victims, Donald Kenrick attains that there are around 10,000 people of Irish Traveller descent living in the USA today.[20] Most of these are thought to be descendants of those who left Ireland in the mid to late nineteenth century. In terms of their history therefore, it is known that emigration was as key to Travellers of the age as was to the rest of Irish society.

It was arguably in the early years of the twentieth century that the nomadic groups, such as Travellers, became more noticeable, as Irish society progressed politically, socially and economically. Aoife Bhreatnach, in her *Becoming Conspicuous: Irish Travellers, Society and State,* goes back as far as 1910, where in the *Irish Independent,* Maurice V. Reidy spoke of "Gypsies in Ireland, differentiating them from Irish tinkers, who lead a somewhat similar wandering life".[21] Travellers were referred to, in national publications as far back as one hundred years ago (See McCormick: 1907; MacNeill: 1919), for example). Up until the twentieth century, it seems Travellers were not spoken about in the somewhat derogatory terms that became apparent as the century wore on. It seems that Travellers were not a "problem" for the state until upwards of one hundred years ago. They worked in harmony with settled people, as tradesmen, musicians, fairground entertainers and some of the other profession mentioned earlier. This "harmony" was though, as Bhreathnach declares, "disrupted by sudden social and economic change that destroyed craft skills and forced Travellers to live in undignified urban squalor".[22] In this context, the industrialisation and progression of Ireland in the early twentieth century was the significant turning point in the history of the Irish Traveller; the point at which they depart from being worthwhile and needed members of society to becoming obsolete in progressive society. In the new Irish state consequently, Irish Travellers were maligned and marginalised from the beginning. They became no longer a presence on

---

[20] Donald Kenrick, "The Travellers of Ireland", *The Patrin Web Journal,* 1 March 1998.

[21] Aoife Bhreatnach, *Becoming Conspicuous: Irish Travellers, Society and State 1922-1970* (Dublin, 2006) p.7.

[22] Ibid, p.8.

Irish roads, and in, or near, communities. Rather, they became a problem, something which needed to be dealt with. As Helleiner explains, a 'Catholic bourgeois nationalism' rather encapsulated the country post-1916, and this "rise of bourgeois nationalism has been identified as significant for understanding the trajectory of anti-Traveller racism".[23] At the dawn of the century, with the initial rise of cultural nationalism and the Irish Literary Revival, Travellers, or 'tinkers' as they would have been referred to, played a somewhat important role, as they were seemingly representative of 'Old Ireland', the pre-colonial state. By the early 1920s, this had given way to 'bourgeois nationalism'. Bhreatnach states, "The marginalisation of Travellers should be placed in the context of the evolution of a civic society".[24] Thus, the developmental nature of early twentieth century Ireland left Travellers estranged and marginalised, casting them to the fringes of society, where there have remained ever since.

Several government acts were passed in the early years of the state, aimed at settling and civilising apparently "uncivilised" groups. The School Attendance Act and the Street Trading Act of 1926[25], although not referring to Travellers directly, affected them most. While it seems these laws were not often directly abided by, their wider social implications regarding public space and family organisation had far-reaching implications for the Travelling community. Pádraig MacGréine became the first folklorist to collect information directly from Travellers, in the 1930s.[26] In light of this, he was perhaps the first person in the 'quest' to empower Travellers by allowing them to speak for themselves. By the 1930s, the state mantra was to seek to settle Travellers, as they had become a 'national problem'. MacGréine responded to this by stating, "Leave us our wandering tinkers. House them and they pine; they have no outlet for their restlessness. Why cage a bird? Why civilise a tinker?"[27] This plan of settlement and 'civilisation' dominated state policy until recent years. Interest in Travellers, not just regarding state policy, but in academic circles, was thrust back into the public domain in the 1930s. MacGréine's submissions in *The Journal of the Folklore of Ireland Society* in the early part of the decade were followed by R.A.S. MacAlister's *The Secret Languages of Ireland,* a work which remains the only definitive study of Ireland's 'secret' languages, such as Traveller languages Shelta and

---

[23] Helleiner, p.47.
[24] Bhreatnach, p.43.
[25] Ibid, p.44.
[26] Helleiner, p.47.
[27] Ibid, p.48.

Cant.[28] As the Traveller 'problem' became more dominant in state policy, the Irish Folklore Commission had become more and more interested in Travellers. The main problem within the Commission, and the problem discussed within the main scope if this project, was that the work was carried out by the settled community, with little, if any input from the Travelling community. The Commission acknowledged the separatist nature of Travellers, but gave little credence to the evidence that suggest their separate existence might have included a separate and unique culture.[29] The Irish Travellers, similar to other historically neglected social groups such as Aborigines, have been denied ethnic and cultural rights until recent years. It has only been with the co-operation of oral historians with these groups that they have become part of the historical register, and subsequently have become empowered, to such an extent that they have fought for and earned ethnic status.

The *1952 Tinker Questionnaire* was resonant of attitudes towards Travellers at the time. It was written about Travellers, and conducted to find information about Travellers, but did not involve Travellers. It was therefore a further example of the cultural, bourgeois nationalism mentioned earlier. The opening page of the *Questionnaire* stated;

The Irish Folklore Commission is issuing this questionnaire in the hope that a representative documentation on certain aspects of the tinkers' way of life may be compiled, before it is too late to do so. It relies confidently on your co-operation towards that end and hopes that your assistance will be forthcoming.[30]

This directive was only aimed at the settled community. The *Questionnaire* was an example of the way in which Travellers have been treated and represented in both society and historical discourse; their identity was constructed by others. The *Questionnaire* was designed to inspect and collect as much information as possible about the Traveller way of life "before it is too late".[31] There were over eight hundred pages of material forwarded to the Commission by its various respondents.[32] The fact that the *Questionnaire* was carried out by members of the settled community, and with no direct involvement from Travellers is of some value to the historian. It serves to provide an insight into the historical relationship between the communities at the time, a time of great social and economic change in Ireland. In terms of this relationship, the

---

[28] Ó hAodha, p.20.
[29] Ibid, p.97.
[30] The Irish Folklore Commission, *1952 Tinker Questionnaire*, p.3.
[31] Ibid, p.5.
[32] O hAodha, p.31.

Questionnaire can be viewed as an example of Othering in the history of Irish Traveller, and can be seen as ethnocentric. As Ó hAodha says of the *Tinker Questionnaire,* "Its insistence on the fixed or unchanging nature of certain representations is of necessity historically inaccurate as any scope for the cultural evolution of the people "fixed within such representations is non-existent".[33] The *Questionnaire* thus portrayed a representation of the Travelling community that was both inaccurate, and not of their own making. It was an example of Othering, in terms of, as Said attests in *Orientalism,* the "common human failing to prefer the schematic authority of a text to the disorientations of direct encounters with the human."[34] The necessity of oral history, and the intrinsic role of the oral historian is then quite evident in terms of this.

While attitudes towards Travellers had been changing, and government policy was beginning to become concerned with the Traveller 'problem' throughout the twentieth century, it was not until the 1963 that the first major report of consequence regarding Irish Travellers was conducted. The *Report of the Commission on Itinerancy* was the first official enquiry by the state into the Traveller issue.[35] For the government, the *Report* was primarily concerned with the introduction of a nationwide settlement policy of the Travelling community. It was conducted, however, without any input from the community. It was compiled by non-Travellers, and contained no trace of anthropological or ethnographic study. It also made no reference to ethnicity with respect to Irish Travellers or gave no credence to the role which ideology (see Eagleton: 1991; Healy: 2002; Said: 1993) played in the construction of Travellers their "marginalisation" within the historical record. Given the widespread view of mainstream society that Travellers were descended from those who lost their lands during the Famine, for them it was merely a case of re-settlement. The Report was therefore incredibly short-sighted, but it did thrust the Travelling community into the public eye. It created a different picture of the community - that of Travellers as a neglected and impoverished people".[36] It also arguably thrust Irish Travellers into the historical 'eye', where oral history gave them the opportunity to construct their discourse on their own terms. The *Report* will also be concentrated upon later in this project. As far as the history of the Irish Traveller goes, the 1963 report was a watershed. At the back of E. Sheehan's *Travellers: Citizens of Ireland,* there is an appendix of the history of legislation in relation to

---

[33] Ibid, p.101.
[34] Said, p.93.
[35] Ó hAodha, p.35.
[36] Sharon Gmelch, *Tinkers and Travellers: Ireland's Nomads* (Dublin, 1975) p.7.

Travellers. The first one listed, in chronological order, is the 1963 report. This tells its own story. The second legislative act listed is the *Report of the Travelling People Review Body,* a full two decades later. This act, twenty years after the 1963 report had denied Travellers ethnic rights, "promoted the integration of Travellers into mainstream society without adequately supporting and promoting their cultural identity".[37] Therefore, twenty years and several governments later, nothing had changed. Travellers were still denied ethnic and cultural rights. The 1983 report however somewhat recognised the Travelling people's "distinctive way of life and identity"[38], but still denied ethnic status, and continued to support absorption. By the 1980s, although, as mentioned, nothing had changed, attitudes arguably were beginning to. As Helleiner asserts, "The 1983 Review Body's references to Traveller identity and tradition exemplified this shift while retaining a commitment to Traveller settlement a necessary to Irish modernisation".[39] In light of this, settlement was still the government mantra, but a slight change in attitude witnessed the recognition of a Traveller identity to an extent. It was well over a decade later that Traveller identity was finally, and officially, recognised.

The latter part of the twentieth century witnessed a large shift towards the empowerment of the Travelling community. Some of the reports and acts passed will be discussed in later chapters. The key report was arguably the 1995 *Report on the Task Force of the Travelling Community,* which made numerous recommendations, and acknowledged the distinct culture and identity of the Traveller community.[40] This report paved the way for recognition as an ethnic minority. Oral history has provided the platform for this empowerment of Irish Travellers. In recent years, Travellers have been able to enter historical discourse, on their own terms, thanks to oral testimony, which has given 'a voice to the voiceless'. The 1990s, and early twenty-first century have led to major breakthroughs in creating their history and preserving and empowering the culture of the Travelling People. The sensationalist nature of the Irish media has not been as kind to the Travelling community as the history and sociology 'industries' have been though. As is the case with many historically and socially neglected groups, the media aims to portray them negatively most of the time. Groups such as Irish Travellers, Roma and Aborigines have had to endure constant negative public images due to the media, as historians attempt to empower them and their cultures concurrently. As

---

[37] Sheehan, p.212.
[38] Helleiner, p.99.
[39] Ibid, p.100.
[40] Sheehan, p.213.

oral history has enabled change and growth for such groups, negative media has attempted to hold them back, while only concentrating on a minority, within minorities. Until these attitudes change, Travellers will continue to be marginalised in Irish society.

Irish Travellers – the Ward family pictured in Portlaoise, County Laois, Ireland. *(P. Harrison Collection)*

3.3 The history of Australian Aborigines

The history of Australian Aborigines draws many and forthright comparisons with Irish Travellers. The main comparison of course is that they have no documented history. Therefore, the history of Aborigines, like Travellers, is a history of history, so to speak. The main comparisons will be discussed in the next chapter. The history of Australia is, primarily, a white history. However, Australia's indigenous people were not white. As far as the traditional historical record goes, its history began in 1788. The problem for its indigenous race was, in that year Australia became a multi-racial country without them being consulted.[41] In Australia, the "historic period" is from the time of white settlement, 1788.[42] Comparatively with the Irish Travelling community, the 1960s were an important decade regarding the history, and therefore empowerment of the Aboriginal people. As Maria Nugent states in her essay on Aboriginal heritage,

Since the late 1960s, a historical silence about the racial structure that shaped Australian society from the moment of first European settlement in 1788, has been replaced by an interest in learning about Aborigines and their relations with colonisers.[43]

Malcolm Prentis agrees, stating, "Until the 1960s, most Australian historians and writers of text-books had virtually ignored the place of Aborigines in Australian history."[44] Similarly to the Travelling community, traditional historical narrative, of which there was hardly any, gave way to a generation of interest for oral historians, anthropologists, ethnographers and sociologists. The Aboriginal voice became heard, and the wrongs of the past came to be somewhat addressed.

It is as difficult to trace the origins of the Aborigine as it is that of the Traveller. Both are a nomadic, wandering race without a sense of linear history, or even time. The oldest Aboriginal remains found in Australia were dated by scientists at more than 60,000 years old.[45] Aborigines, arguably therefore, have been around for many thousands of years. As mentioned, the Aboriginal race has no concept of linear time, making it extremely hard to estimate a time of arrival in Australia. Aborigines believe in the concept of Dreamtime. This can be loosely defined as the time of creation, where the heavens and Earth were one. For Aborigines, the Dreamtime created heaven, Earth and the people as three different parts that should never be divided.[46] .The concept of Aboriginal 'dreamtime' displays further the historical problem. To create a history, as close to the truth as possible, remains increasingly difficult for a culture, a people, who have no sense of chronological time. As eminent Australian historian Stuart Macintyre states, "This 'dreamtime', synonymous with the Aboriginals, is not fixed chronologically, since it spans the past and the

---

[41] Malcolm Prentis, *A Study in Black and White: The Aborigines in Australian History* (Sydney, 1975) p.1.
[42] Maria Nugent, "Mapping Memories", in Paula Hamilton and Linda Shopes (eds.), *Oral History and Public Memories* (Philadelphia, 2008) p.49.
[43] Ibid, p.47.
[44] Prentis, p.4.
[45] Richard Nile, *Australian Aborigines* (Illinois, 1993) p.4.
[46] Ibid, p.6.

present to carry an enduring meaning".[47] Therefore, in the Aboriginal psyche, the people were created by the land and could not survive without it. This makes the estimation of Aboriginal arrival, and indeed a creation of any historical construct very difficult. Oral historians have had to overcome that barrier in their attempts to document Aboriginal history. The documentation and construction of a realistic, evidence-based Australian history has been therefore difficult, if not impossible, to the point where debate has as much been about the nature of history rather than the history itself. For Australian's, Aborigines inclusive, these debates have caused so much consternation that they are known as the 'History Wars'. In this way, rather than focusing on a history of the Aborigine itself, twentieth and twenty-first century Australian history has focused on arguing the extent of historical truth to be gained from oral testimony regarding the Aboriginal people.

3.3.1 Historical Representations of the Aboriginal people: Australia's 'History Wars'

The quest to obtain the history of the Aborigine in Australia has tended to encompass arguing historians and politicians than the search for truth. Leading Aboriginal historian, Bain Attwood questions "Is history a science or an art? Whose knowledge is history? For what purposes is history told? To whom are historians responsible?"[48] These are the questions at the very root of the Australian 'History Wars', at the heart of the attempted construction of Aboriginal history. The Prime Minister of Australia from 1993 to 1996, Paul Keating stated in an article written in 2003, "History is always our most useful tool and guide. Knowing our past helps us to divine our future".[49] For Aborigines, this is not possible, not in documented discourse at least. The 'History Wars' though have proven to not have been steeped principally in history. It has been quite evident that the whole situation has occurred within a political context. The 'History Wars' flared up particularly around the time of the Australian bi-centenary, where the slogan "White Australia has a black history"[50] became popular and widespread. The 'History Wars' have been played out in political circles for many years now in Australia, and were often the

---

[47] Stuart Macintyre, *A Concise History of Australia*, (Melbourne, 2004) p.16.

[48] Bain Attwood, *Telling the Truth about Aboriginal History*, (New South Wales, 2005) p.4.

[49] Paul Keating, "Reflections on the History Wars: The political battle for Australia's future", in *Online Opinion*, 12 September 2003.

[50] Attwood, p.25.

main source of argument and debate in the 1990s between liberal P.M., Paul Keating, and his conservative predecessor, John Howard. Greg Melleuish, in a recent article in *The Australian,* alludes to this, stating

> For them, history is about alternately cheering and booing the past. This was, in fact, the starting point for the history wars. Some historians in the 1970s and 80s forgot that their role was to inquire into the past and provide as accurate a view of it as possible. For them history was the handmaiden of politics, to be used to support contemporary causes.[51]

The 'them' mentioned refers to those historians (and politicians) whose arguments had been the only real representation of the Aborigine in history up to the last decade of the twentieth century. What then of these 'Wars' in their correct context; history? The main protagonist of the 'History Wars', Keith Windschuttle, who as Attwood indicates, has been become a minor celebrity rather than a widely credited historian during the debacle, says that another of the main historians involved, Stuart Macintyre, in his work *The History Wars,*[52] "divides people into goodies and baddies, and the goodies are those who support Paul Keating, and the bad historians are the ones who claim support to John Howard"[53]. History, therefore, has played a monumental role in Australian politics in recent years, indeed in Australian life itself. The 'History Wars' erupted primarily due to Keith Windschuttle, and his views on the 'false history' that he believed had been written regarding the atrocities and genocide against the indigenous Australians at the time of colonisation. Windschuttle said of previous documented history, on the talk show "Lateline", in 2003, "the whole thing could not be sustained by evidence".[54] Evidence is the key to history. To create an Aboriginal history, oral testimony, the only type of 'evidence' which can be used directly regarding the Aboriginal race, has been the key. For conservative historians such as Windschuttle, this testimony has been discredited. Where then has this left Aboriginal history?

The debate arose from arguments over the extent of the genocide, which occurred in the late eighteenth and nineteenth centuries at the hands of the British settlers. Windschuttle argues that the extent of the violence was extremely low. Historians such as Stuart Macintyre and Henry Reynolds argue quite different points, that the colonisation of Australia,

---

[51] Greg Melleuish, "Leave History Alone", *The Australian,* 1 September 2009
[52] Stuart Macintyre, *The History Wars,* (Melbourne, 2003).
[53] Tony Jones, "Authors in History Debate: Macintyre and Windschuttle", on *Lateline,* Australian Broadcasting Corporation, 3 September 2003.
[54] Ibid.

beginning in 1788, was marred by exploitation, dispossession and atrocities against the natives. The fact of the matter regarding the 'History Wars' is that Australian history was, and is, incomplete. (See Scates: 1997; Povinelli: 1992; Parkes: 2007). As Stuart Macintyre says, "the older history noticed Aborigines only as a tragic and disturbing presence, victims of iron law and progress (...) the Aborigines were deemed to lack a history of their own".[55] Consequently, the difficulties in creating an Aboriginal history become apparent, particularly when the actual creation of an historical construct is in itself such an argumentative issue. Similarly to Irish Travellers, the documented history of the Aboriginal people is blighted by arguing factions, and arguably the divide between traditional and oral historians.

As previously mentioned, one of main protagonists of the 'History Wars' has been conservative historian Keith Windschuttle. His assertion, in works such as *The Fabrication of Aboriginal History*, that the atrocities and genocide, at the time of colonisation in Australia, were generally not true, has been the principle argument in these debates. One of Windschuttle's main adversaries in the debacle is the also aforementioned Stuart Macintyre, one of Australia's best known historians. Macintyre states that Keith Windschuttle asserted the frontier massacres are a myth invented by "self serving humanitarians and perpetuated by dishonest intellectuals."[56] Another of the leading oral historians in the field, Bain Attwood, has widely discredited Windschuttle, in publications such as *Telling the Truth about Aboriginal History*. Attwood arguably attests that the 'History Wars' are, indeed, the result of oral history versus traditional history. He states "Windschuttle has argued the treatment of the Aboriginal people at the frontiers of white settlement amounts to a fabrication".[57] For Attwood, the Windshuttlian viewpoint is one created by a generation of politically inspired, traditional academic historians. He maintains that in the eyes of the colonising British, the Aborigines were an almost obsolete race and as an ancient people, they belonged to the confines of anthropology, not history.[58] In truth, they belong to both, in terms of oral history's interdisciplinary nature. It is particularly unfortunate for the Aboriginal people, that attempts at creating a historical discourse had, until recently, become centred on warring historians. In the absence of clear, objective history, which is difficult in terms of this situation, allegiances have mainly either sided with Windschuttle or his rivals, such

---

[55] Macintyre, *The History Wars,* p.9.

[56] Ibid, p.59.

[57] Attwood, p.2.

[58] Ibid, p.16.

as Macintyre and Henry Reynolds. As previously stated, the 'war' has been twinned with politics. Therefore politics has, and will always, play an intrinsic role in history and historiography. The opposing views of Keating and Howard in the 'History Wars' lay further claim to this. Another of the most important figures in the 'wars' is Henry Reynolds. Reynolds has been a primary figure in a vital shift in the concept of Aboriginal history, playing an intrinsic role in landmark Aboriginal cases, such as the Eddie Mabo case in June 1992, where Mabo was awarded land as part of the ongoing Aboriginal land rights battle.

Reynolds was a "target" of Windschuttle's during the course of the 'History War' debates. (See Moran: 2002). He is an advocate of land rights for Aboriginal communities, seeing it as critical to righting the wrongs of the past.[59] Similarly to Macintyre and Attwood, Reynolds has been a staunch opponent of Windschuttle and his followers. As Reynolds says in his review of Windschuttle's *Fabrication*, "the black armbands can come off and go in the rubbish (…) If anyone should say sorry for the past, it's the Aborigines, whose criminal ancestors behaved so badly towards the white pioneers".[60] Reynolds mockingly veiled attack on Windschuttle shows the divisive nature of the differing viewpoints in the 'History Wars'. Reynolds, therefore, is a huge advocate of Aboriginal rights, a believer in the 'black armband view', i.e. the view that focuses on the wrongdoing of the British settlers during colonisation. However, as mentioned, viewpoint is paramount in cases such as this, and as Geoffrey Partington points out in his essay on Reynolds, "It is unfair of Reynolds to condemn British explorers and colonists over a century ago for failing to comprehend customs relating to land usage in traditional Aboriginal society".[61] Partington though, as Macintyre points out in *The History Wars,* "was a South Australian academic and History Warrior who championed Australia's British origins" [62], while asserting that Partington published the work to attempt to show Reynolds was misleading in his land rights campaign. Reynolds views must be seen objectively, but as previously stated, in situations where no written records of history exist, objectivity is not easy to achieve. The notion of rights became highly relevant though with the Eddie Mabo case. The Mabo case turned the idea of 'terra nullius', which Windschuttle believed to be fabrication, on its

---

[59] Nick Beams, "What is at stake in Australia's History Wars?", in *World Socialist Web Site,* 16 July 2004.
[60] Ibid.
[61] Geoffrey Partington, *The Australian History of Henry Reynolds,* (Adelaide, 1994) p.8.
[62] Macintyre, *The History Wars,* p.144.

head. Mabo's collaboration with historians, especially Henry Reynolds, helped him to lay claim to the land, and helped write Aboriginals into history. Frank Welsh says in his *A New History of Australia*, that the decision to grant land to the Aborigines would have a very restricted impact, but that the Aboriginal claim to participate in "that most fundamental of principles, the disposal of land, which had aroused so much indignation, was firmly established".[63] In light of this, the history of the Aboriginal had not been altered beyond all comprehensible belief, but had been changed in a way that future change could be achieved. Reynolds became, especially after Mabo, the recognised authority on Aboriginal land rights[64] due to his friendship and close collaboration with Eddie Mabo, who in fact died before the verdict was made. If not a turning point, then the Mabo case was a cross on the road to a turning point in recent years for Australia's indigenous people and an intrinsic case in the nature of the varying viewpoints tied up in the complex 'History Wars'. The 'History Wars', and in particular the Mabo case of 1992, demonstrate both the need for and ability of oral history and testimony in relation to those socially and historically neglected groups.

Henry Reynolds' works *Dispossession* and *Frontier* display the necessary constituents in constructing Aboriginal history, indeed the facets of the documentation of any historically neglected group. He uses a combination of source material and his own collected oral testimony. While having his oral work with the likes of Mabo gained land rights and native title for Aborigines, his collected source material portrays the reality of the 'frontier', the time of white colonial settlement, an example of which is taken from a letter from a young Englishman, Henry Mort to his mother and sister in 1844,

> Had a very animated discussion on the 'Moral Right of a Nation to take forcible possession of a County inhabited by savages'. John and David McConnell argued that it is morally right for a Christian nation to extirpate savages from their native soil in order that it may be peopled with a more intelligent and civilised race of human beings. Fr. McConnell and myself were of the opposite opinion and argued that a nation had no moral right to take forcible possession of any place.[65]

---

[63] Frank Welsh, *Great Southern Land: A New History of Australia,* (London, 2004) p.542.

[64] Ibid, p.541.

[65] Henry Mort, "Letter to his mother and sister, Cressbrook, 28 January 1844", in Henry Reynolds, *Dispossesion: Black Australians and White Invaders* (New South Wales, 1989) p.4.

This statement represents the essence of colonialism and dispossession, which both Aborigines and Irish Travellers were subjected to at the hands of colonial Britain. As mentioned, therefore histories of both have not been represented in subsequent 'national' histories. Oral history has attempted to fill this representational void.

In terms of oral history and the role of the oral historian, the relationship between truth and history is no more apparent than in these Australian 'History Wars'. It is the position of the historian, in essence, to be objective and to attempt to provide an empirical history. However, it is very rare, perhaps impossible, for a historian to be entirely objective. As Windschuttle says "the responsibility of the historian is not to be compassionate, it is to be dispassionate. What the historians of Aboriginal Australia have done is they've taken sides in disputes".[66] It raises the question of objectivity to new levels, and the question can objective truth ever really be obtained in history, particularly history from below. The fact that there is no written Aboriginal history, or record of any kind, makes a linear Aboriginal history almost impossible, the key factor in the 'History Wars'. Politics has a lot to do with this lack of objectivity and truth. There is no such thing as a non-political or value free history, as can also be seen in the history of Irish Travellers. Every historian has a political outlook.[67] This in terms of people such as Windschuttle, Attwood, Reynolds and Macintyre, himself a former member of the Communist party, strengthens the point at the heart of the 'History Wars'- objective truth in history. Macintyre has been said to be progressive in outlook, acknowledging the achievements of Australia, but recognising the crimes of the past. Windschuttle on the other hand, could not be said to be progressive, rather conservative. Neither though could be said to be entirely objective, or to have created an empirical history of Australia, as can be said of Reynolds, Geoffrey Blainey and Manning Clark, amongst others. In this case, it is almost impossible. Australia is, arguably, being constantly dragged down by the crimes of the past, whether they happened similarly to how they have been written as Macintyre and Reynolds would state, or whether they are a Windschuttlian myth. Therefore, while oral testimonies have led to the documentation of Aboriginal history, and in turn their social empowerment, it has raised nationwide questions in Australia about objectivity and validity. It seems in this case that the re-evaluation of history has led to acrimony, and very varying versions of the truth. Therefore, as mentioned before, it is almost impossible to find the objective

---

[66] Jones, p.2.
[67] Beams, p.2.

truth in Australian history, no less in the complex history of a "two hundred year old" state.

It is unfortunate for the Aboriginal race that their pursuit of a documented history has become instead a media playground of warring historians. Similarly to that of Irish Travellers, the history of the Aboriginal race concerns historians talking about and debating it, rather than actually documenting it, until recent years. Oral historians have endeavoured to change this, and the likes of Reynolds and Attwood in particular have worked closely with Aborigines. Statements from the likes of Keith Windschuttle, such as "The colonial authorities wanted to civilise and modernise the Aborigines, not exterminate them. Their intentions were not to foster violence towards the Aborigines"[68] would appear to go against most Aboriginal testimony of the time. Like Irish Travellers, the Aboriginal race has suffered from cultural legitimacy with regard to the British settlers, those whom Windschuttle defends, "Aboriginal and settler Australian's have a common problem: a lack of legitimacy. Their moral status, and hence, their identities and rights are denied by the other group."[69] The contentious nature of the divide between the 'warring' historical factions has meant that the actual construction of Aboriginal history had suffered throughout the later twentieth century. The ability and popularity of oral history in the present day means that Aboriginal rights and history, like that of its comparative counterpart, the Irish Travelling community, finally have a platform and have led to the social empowerment of the groups. The construction and documentation of histories of the groups have led to them being able to look forward to a much brighter future.

---

[68] Attwood, p.89
[69] Ibid, p.190

CHAPTER FOUR

HISTORY AS STRUGGLE: REPRESENTATIONAL COMPARISONS

4.1 Comparative Cultures, Comparative Problems

The lifestyles, cultures and histories of the indigenous groups of Ireland and Australia are thus very similar. Quite clearly there are also many differences, but for the scope of this project, the many comparisons have and will be concentrated on. The dominant comparison mentioned throughout so far has been that there is no documented history of either group. They have been the victims of Othering, victims of an institutionalised, hegemonic view of history in their respective countries. They are both indigenous to their native lands, have both been victims of colonisation, have been socially neglected and have been the constant victims of stereotypes. They have both seen their populations decrease significantly, and currently occupy only very small percentages of their country's populations. Both groups have suffered at the hands of their governments, and have been victims of forced assimilation and resettlement, or as the Travellers themselves would see it, simply settlement. Representation in history has always been for them, and never by them. They are both comparable in terms of poorer average health in comparison with the settled populations, tend to be less educated and tend to be constantly portrayed negatively in the media. Oral history, and its aforementioned ability to give a voice to these communities, has enabled them to attempt to, at least, give their side of the story. As Perks and Thompson explain, oral history allows for the "empowerment of individuals or social groups through the process of remembering and re-interpreting the past".[1] This "re-interpreting" has been the vital constituent in the enabling and empowerment of the Australian Aborigine and the Irish Traveller. This chapter will provide a comparative analysis of both, particularly regarding media representation, colonialism, assimilation and

---

[1] Perks and Thompson, p.9.

later twentieth century developments, all with reference to some of the latest theoretics in these subject areas (see Benjamin et al.:2002; Lahcens, 2003).

4.2 Negative Media Portraits

A continuous and major comparative problem for both the Travelling and Aboriginal people has been their negative portrayal in the media in their respective countries. While traditional historical representations have been less than kind to both groups, media representations, both in the past and present have certainly attributed to their marginalisation. Consistently Travellers and Aborigines have been denigrated as lazy and troublesome, as criminals, alcoholics and deviants, both on television and in print media. Similar to representations of them in history, media representations of the groups are never conducted by members of the groups. Othering therefore is an almost omnipresent presence, not just present in academic practices, but pervading all walks of life for maligned social groups.

The Irish media is a multi-million euro industry. In terms of the media, Irish Travellers are a group who, perhaps, are the least equipped to 'fight' this industry, in the sphere of Irish society. The low literacy levels of the community, and subsequently their low level of public, media of historical representatives make it near impossible to defend against the media, and therefore has led to the creation of deeply entrenched stereotypes. As Jack Fennell states in his "How to make a Folk Devil", news tends to highlight issues that concern the upper and middle classes.[2] Traveller representations are, arguably more often than not, negative in the media. The figure of the Traveller, and especially the Traveller-trader, in the Irish media, is "that of a rogue, a con-man, whose activities take place in a moral and legal grey area[3]. Fennell, in his essay, accuses Eamon Dillon, who is the leading correspondent on Traveller related crime for the tabloid *Sunday World*, and by so, many other contributors to media representations of the Travelling community, of almost exonerating the media in creating a Traveller mistrust, rather blaming Travellers themselves for both creating a fear of them, and for themselves having a total lack of trust for the settled community. This is certainly the case in many situations. Travellers, quite easy targets for languid, easy journalism become maligned in print and on

---

[2] Jack Fennell, "How to make a Folk Devil: Travellers and 'True Crime' Literaure" in O hAodha, M. (ed.), *On the Margins of Memory: Recovering the Migrant Voice,* (Newcastle, 2007) p. 99.
[3] Ibid, p. 103.

screen, when in many cases it is overwhelmingly unwarranted. However, to borrow the term again, there is a 'grey area'. For all the innocent Travellers, superfluous victims of deep rooted bias in society, there are many more involved in crime, which deserve their negative place on screen and in print. A few months ago, newspapers carried stories of Traveller scams in places as diverse as Iceland, and the other country at the heart of this study, Australia. In Australia, a group of up to fifty travellers, selling faulty generators, were caught when a television 'sting' caught two of them on camera selling the generators. Australian publication, the *Irish Echo,* stated "the group originates from the Rathkeale area of Limerick and its individuals operate under the names Quilligan and Sheridan".[4] Sheridan and Quilligan are well-known Traveller families in Ireland. Situations like these make it incredibly hard for members of the settled community to trust the Travelling community, and it is unfortunate that reports similar to this occur almost weekly in the Irish media. The mistrust of the settled community towards its Travelling counterparts was devastatingly evident in the 2005 Padraig Nally case. Nally, having killed Traveller John Ward, was found guilty of manslaughter in November 2005, before being acquitted in October 2006.[5] A Pavee Point press release stated "If John Ward was not a Traveller, would Padraig Nally be walking free tonight".[6] This case clearly demonstrated the deep, entrenched divide almost inbuilt in Irish society, with Travellers claiming murder, and the settled community claiming self-defence. It is these types of situations, and in particular media involvement, which help create and widen these divides. Whereas many Travellers do their community no favours within the confines of mainstream media, there are many more who are seemingly innocent victims. Unfortunately for the Irish Travelling community, their lack of representation at both historical and social level has led to this marginalisation. Oral historians have therefore attempted to plot the community on a historical course, creating a past, whereby they may be able to represent themselves academically in the future. This entrenches the notion of oral history's ability to give a voice to those without.

---

[4] *Irish Echo Online*, "Net tightens on rogue traders after TV sting", 7 November 2008.
[5] *RTE News,* "Nally conviction quashed, retrial ordered", 12 November 2006.
[6] *Pavee Point,* "Pavee Point Press Release: Nally Acquittal", 14 December 2006.

Irish Traveller Liam Riley from County Kilkenny, Ireland. The Irish Travellers, similar to the rest of the Irish people have always had a great love of horses. (*P. Harrison Collection*).

Comparatively, the Aboriginal community in Australia have suffered at the hands of its country's media. Aboriginal history and Aboriginal media representation already have an intrinsic link, in that the previously mentioned 'History Wars' have been played out in the media itself. They thrust both the historian and the subject into the spotlight in recent decades. Therefore, from the very outset, Aboriginal history and representation was media-dominated. Apart from this though, the Aboriginal community have suffered a strikingly similar fate to that of the Travelling community in the media, being portrayed negatively and maligned for the most part. Michael Meadows states in *Voices in the Wilderness,* "The forces behind misrepresentation are powerful ones".[7] They are clearly much more powerful than the Aboriginal race itself, and so it is, and has been, the occupation of the oral historian to create representation. Meadows goes on to assert, in relation to misrepresentation, that following an extensive study of over two thousand newspaper articles

[7] Michael Meadows, *Voices in the Wilderness: Images of Aboriginal People in the Australian Media* (Connecticut, 2001) p.49.

dealing with Aboriginal issues in Australia, that the "dominating news value was Aboriginal involvement with the criminal justice system".[8] At the centre of the debate on Aboriginal history has been the notion of objectivity and truth. This notion of truth must also apply to the Australian media. As Hartley and McKee state, "In such a context, the status of journalism simply cannot survive unscathed, nor has it. Just as science, reason, and truth have attracted sustained criticism, so must journalism".[9] Consequently, as the question of truth has had to be questioned by historians in Australia, it is only just that it should be taken into account by the media, where it largely has not. Meadows relays the representational struggles of the Aborigine in the media back to the Australian bi-centenary in 1988. He states that "Of the nine Aboriginal people who were allowed to comment directly on the meaning of 26 January, four appeared on *SBS News,* three on *ABC News* and the other two were on *National Nine News.* But just four Aboriginal spokespeople were identified by name in the stories used."[10] The Aboriginal representatives, most of them at least, were not deemed important enough to be given titles, rather in terms of the media coverage, they were arguably lucky to be represented in the first place, especially in a positive fashion. In recent years, with the large coverage of the granting of land rights, positive reporting of Aborigines has increased, due chiefly to the ability of oral history and testimony in earning native title in the first place. In this way, oral historians have enabled empowerment of the race, in their collaborative efforts to represent them.

---

[8] Ibid, p.49.
[9] John Hartley and Alan McKee, *The Indigenous Public Sphere: The Reporting and Reception of Indigenous Issues in the Australian Media, 1994-1997* (New York, 2000) p.31.
[10] Meadows, p.83.

Group of Aboriginal Adults and Children.[11]

"Written in a Face" – Elderly Irish Traveller woman Maggie has lived an
interesting life. *(P. Harrison Collection).*

---

[11] A sincere thank you to http://www.mediaman.com.au/profiles/githabul_people
.html for this image. (Accessed 10/12/2010).

4.3 Colonialism-Social groups subject to enforced change

The colonial pasts of both Ireland and Australia are well documented. Ireland struggled under British colonial rule for centuries, and documented Australian history only begins with the British 'conquest' of 1788. Is the historically neglected status, marginalisation and 'Othering' of Aborigines and Travellers a consequence of colonisation? Is it a coincidence that they are both maligned groups in post-colonial nations? It arguably is not, particularly for the indigenous Australians. Australia was not a land of terra nullius[12], "a land that until its settlement in 1788 lacked human habitation, law, government or history".[13] It certainly contained all those things, but not in their Western terms. When Captain Cook sailed the eastern coast, named it New South Wales and claimed possession on it in the name of his monarch[14], Aboriginal life would never be the same again. Ann McGrath puts in quite simply in *Contested Ground;* "Australian history can be summarised as the story of how Aboriginal people lost a continent, and how the invaders gained one."[15] Former Australian Prime Minister, Paul Keating said, in one of the most famous speeches in Australian history, at Redfern, Sydney in 1992;

> It begins, I think, with an act of recognition. Recognition that it was we who did the dispossessing. We took the traditional lands and smashed the traditional way of life. We brought the diseases. The alcohol. We committed the murders. We took the children from their mothers. We practised discrimination and exclusion. It was our ignorance and our prejudice. And our failure to imagine these things being done to us.[16]

Redfern is a place where the Aboriginal people have established their communities in defiance of non-Aboriginals. It is a magnet for Aborigines from all over Australia when they visit Sydney. As a consequence of British colonisation, the Aboriginal people lost their way of life. In terms of the previously mentioned 'History Wars', with the atrocities that occurred at the hands of the British being questioned, what then accounts for the rapid destruction of a race? The impact of colonisation of the Aboriginal race was immense, and destructive. No more than a few years

---

[12] Terra Nullius meant unoccupied land, and was the legally endorsed premise of the British occupation of Australia.
[13] Macintyre, *A Concise History of Australia,* p.5.
[14] Ibid, p.1.
[15] Ann McGrath, *Contested Ground: Australian Aborigines under the British Crown* (New South Wales, 1995) p.1.
[16] Attwood, p.28.

after entering the country, Britain was using Australia as a veritable dumping ground for its criminals, and that of its other colonies. As Patrick O' Farrell attests, in *The Irish in Australia*, "The first convicts sent direct from Ireland- 133 males and 22 females- arrived from Cork on the 26th September 1791. By the 1820s, such Irish convicts were arriving at an average rate of about 1000 a year."[17] Therefore, while attributing gravely to the destruction of the indigenous people of their new-found colony, they then filled the colony with as many criminals as they could send. McGrath states that in the short and long term, "colonialism drastically jeopardised the personal liberty of Aborigines."[18] For her, the British came, and the Aboriginal people suffered, greatly.

The people of Ireland suffered a similar fate, at the hands of British colonisation. The Irish were a marginalised race for centuries, and Irish Travellers became a marginalised 'race within a race', so to speak. Christine Walsh states, regarding postcolonial legacy, that "the racist rhetoric depicting Travellers as an 'aberrant' people closely emulates more generic English attitudes towards the Irish people as a whole under colonial rule".[19] Therefore, the Travelling community became the 'other' within an 'other', due to the denigration of the Irish people in general at the hands of British colonial rule. Regarding representation during colonial rule, Travellers are virtually invisible, as Míchael Ó hAodha confirms, "The colonial tradition made no distinction between Travellers and other Irish people with the result that they are largely invisible in the historical record".[20] In this way, Travellers suffered a kind of 'double jeopardy', faced with the problem of both being Irish, and being members of a maligned group within Irish society. The guise of colonialism was the need to 'civilise' and settle seemingly uncivilised peoples. The Irish represented this for the British. However, Travellers represented this for the Irish. The Travelling community therefore had to contend with problems from both sides, and were represented by neither.

4.4 Government Attempts to "Fix" Indigenous Groups

For the respective governments of Ireland and Australia, Travellers and Aborigines have long been 'problem' groups. Their indigenous status has meant very little to various governments, and their attempts at 'fixing'

---

[17] Patrick O' Farrell, *The Irish in Australia: 1788 to the Present* (Cork, 2001) p.23
[18] McGrath, p.2.
[19] Christine Walsh and Míchael Ó hAodha (ed.), *Postcolonial Borderlands: Orality and Irish Traveller Writing* (Newcastle, 2008) p.23.
[20] Ó hAodha, p.92.

these problems, in the past, were carried out with little or no involvement from the groups themselves. At the heart of comparable government policy to 'fix' the groups was settlement and assimilation. For the purpose of this section, two government–based programs will be concentrated on. In Ireland, the 1963 *Report of the Commission on Itinerancy* laid down plans for Traveller settlement, without representation. The Stolen Generations in Australia is the name given to the government policy of taking Aboriginal children from their families and 'settling' them with white parents.

4.4.1 The 1963 Report of the Commission on Itinerancy

By the 1960s, the Travelling community were becoming a problem for the Irish government. As Ireland became more urbanised, Travellers tended to move closer to towns and cities. This created problems, as George Gmelch, states "such as trespassing, littering and damage caused by wandering horses".[21] Thus, as Helleiner attests, the formation of the Commission on Itinerancy in 1960 was "clearly responding to increased pressure from local authorities, especially in urban areas".[22] The Report, in 1963, used to word 'itinerant' to refer to Travellers, or people "who had no fixed abode and habitually wandered from place to place."[23] There was no mention of status, ethnic or otherwise, and there was no involvement of or with any members of the Travelling community, in what can be termed as a landmark document in their relatively undocumented history. They were simply grouped as itinerants, without any status, and in need of settlement and rehabilitation. As the Report itself states,

> Itinerants (or travellers as they prefer to be called) do not constitute a single homogenous group, tribe or community within the nation, although the settled population are inclined to regard them as such. Neither do they constitute a separate ethnic group.[24]

John O' Connell states, in a 1998 press release for *Pavee Point*, that the 1963 report was the first phase of a "clear and explicit government response to the Travellers in Ireland"[25], the second phase of which was the

---

[21] George Gmelch, *The Irish Tinkers: The Urbanisation of an Itinerant People,* (Illinois, 1985) p.51.

[22] Helleiner, p.75.

[23] *Report of the Commission on Itinerancy,* (Dublin, 1963) p.13.

[24] Ibid, p.37.

[25] John O' Connell, "Travellers in Ireland: An Examination of Discrimination and Racism", *Pavee Point Travellers Centre,* January 1998, p.1.

1983, *Report of the Travelling People Review Body.* Firstly, as O' Connell
says, the 1963 report was a 'response' by the government to the Traveller
problem. However, Travellers had been roaming the island for centuries,
and had been talked about in government, as well as having been the
subject of legislation since the 1920s. Secondly, this second phase which
O' Connell speaks of did not occur until two decades later. Why then did it
take so long for the government to attempt to 'fix' the Travellers in the
first place, and subsequently why did this 'second phase' take twenty years
to come into place? The obvious answers lie in lack of representation of
the community in both society and history. Also though, the Travelling
community, who had proven so useful to settled population as tradesmen
and entertainers in previous decades, were now becoming obsolete in a
newly urbanised and industrial country. Therefore, instead of trying to
accommodate Travellers as regards their own way of life, they were to be
forced to assimilate and settle into the settled community, against their
will, wishes, culture and society. They were to be 'fixed', in accordance
with findings about their community, but which had no input from their
community. In 1963, traditional history was paramount and the advent of
oral history as a means of documenting and representing neglected social
groups was decades away. The 1963 report was, therefore, incredibly
short-sighted, created by government officials, having researched
information about the Travelling community from the settled population,
from government reports and from local authorities. Nowhere in the
construction or implementation of the report was their input from
Travellers. Ethnic status was a major issue involved with the 1963 report.
Travellers were denied a distinct and separate ethnicity; rather they were
simply referred to as 'itinerants'. In theory the government wished to be
seen as a "fair and progressive protector of all its citizens"[26], but in
observation and practice, it was far from it. Charlie Haughey, who was
parliamentary secretary at the time, stated at the inaugural meeting of the
Commission on Itinerancy, "Of paramount importance is the simple fact
that the humblest itinerant is entitled to a place in the sun and to share in
the benefits of our society".[27] In practice, Travellers would not see any
'place in the sun', and certainly would not share in the benefits of Irish
society at the time. They remained on the margins of Irish life,
unrepresented and undocumented, as various governments attempted to
'fix' them without consulting them. It was not until the last years of the
twentieth century that Travellers began to become more academically and

[26] Helleiner, p.78.
[27] *Report of the Commission on Itinerancy,* p.114.

socially represented, particularly with the 1995 *Report of the Task Force on the Travelling Community,* where their ethnic status was finally recognised. Close collaboration with oral historians allowed Travellers to become represented, documented and recognised, and thus played a significant role in their quest for ethnicity.

4.4.2 The Stolen Generations

The Stolen Generations is the name given to the government policy of removing Aboriginal children from their families and settling them with white families. This policy was designed to ensure that the indigenous Aboriginal race would eventually die out. This formed the Australian government's attempts to 'fix' the Aboriginal 'problem'. It occurred throughout the late nineteenth and twentieth centuries, until it was became officially outlawed in 1969. The inferior and negative stereotypical status of Aborigines meant that most of Australia's settled population were easily convinced by the government that this was the right thing to do for the betterment of the Aboriginal race. For most, a life away from their mother race would be entirely beneficial to Aboriginal children. Therefore, the various Australian governments of the time were able to carry out these unlawful assimilatory measures. It is described in Stuart Macintyre's *The History Wars,* while quoting another eminent Australian historian, Robert Manne as "one of the most shameful, if not *the* most shameful episode in twentieth century Australian history".[28] Macintyre subsequently gives his definition of the Stolen Generations,

> For seventy years state governments had removed children of mixed descent from their Aboriginal parents to merge them into European society. In its most sinister, inter-war phase, when the administrators still expected the 'tribal natives' to die out, it constituted what Manne described as a 'eugenics program of constructive miscegenation' to breed out the colour of the mixed-descent population to solve what was then regarded as 'the Aboriginal problem'[29].

The idea was to breed out the 'problem' race, and to ensure the majority of the population was unrecognisably Aboriginal within a couple of generations. The 'stolen' children, and their subsequent generations were quantified by varying degrees of 'whiteness', such as "'full-blood, 'half-caste', 'quadroon' and 'octoroon'".[30] According to the 1997 *Bringing Them Home* Report, it

---

[28] Macintyre, *The History Wars,* p. 145.
[29] Ibid, p. 145.
[30] Macintyre, *A Concise History of Australia,* p.145.

is not possible to state with any precision how many children were forcibly removed as many records have not survived and others fail to record the children's Aboriginality.[31] The report states though that "we can conclude with confidence that between one and three and one in ten children were forcibly removed from their families and communities between 1910 and 1970, while in certain regions and in certain periods the figure was undoubtedly much greater than one in ten.[32] Historians have estimated that up to 100,000 children were taken between 1910 and 1970. This statistic, however true it may be, is shocking considering by 1901, the Aboriginal population in Australia had fallen to about 100,000.[33] Bain Attwood states, in *Telling the Truth About Aboriginal History,* that as far as British settlers, those who would go on to form Australian governments, were concerned the Aborigines were "either a race doomed to die out or a child race in need of European tutorship".[34] In the colonising mind, evolution meant that the demise of the Aboriginal race was a natural course of events".[35] Clearly, for the settlers who formed subsequent governments, the race did not follow the 'natural course' quick enough. The dispossession of Aboriginal children had almost Nazi overtones, and similarities to the Roma. While the Stolen Generations itself is not the main focus of this study, the testimony of those who suffered certainly is. Shocking figures emerged in the late twentieth century linked to the trauma involved in being 'taken'. Many 'stolen' Aborigines have suffered from mental illness, and many more have related horrific stories of abuse. Rosanne Kennedy, in her essay "Stolen Generations Testimony", indicates the intrinsic connection between oral history and trauma-based history regarding neglected groups, and advocates the "declining status of academic history as the guardian of the 'truth' of the past".[36] The collaboration of oral historians and Aboriginal victims was vital in the construction of the 1997 *Bringing Them Home* report, arguably the greatest landmark document in Aboriginal, and indeed Australian history. The relating of these crimes to oral historians have enabled the truth to be told, and inevitably led to the empowerment of the stolen Aboriginal

---

[31] *Bringing Them Home: National Inquiry into the Separation of Aboriginal and Torres Strait Islander Children from Their Families* (New South Wales, 1997) p.36.
[32] Ibid, p.37.
[33] Attwood, p.159.
[34] Ibid, p.139.
[35] Ibid, p.139.
[36] Rosanne Kennedy, "Stolen Generations Testimony- Trauma, Historiography and the Question of 'Truth'", in Perks and Thomson, *The Oral History Reader,* p.507.

generations. For example, Bain Attwood demonstrates in "Learning about the Truth: The Stolen Generations narrative" how testimony was vital for righting the wrongs of the past, and enabling the Aboriginal race to move forward. An example of testimony in his work is that of Margaret Tucker, who was forcibly removed from her mother on a New South Wales Aboriginal reserve in 1917,

> The people at Cummeroogunga lived in constant fear of their children being sent away from them by the board and being placed in homes. Wholesale kidnapping occurred on the Mission. The Manager sent the Aboriginal men away on a rabbiting expedition. No sooner had they left the station then carloads of police (who had been waiting) dashed in and seized all the children they could get their hands on. The children were bundled into the cars and taken away for the Board to dispose of. Many of them never saw their parents again.[37]

Testimony such as this demonstrates the atrocities carried on, not only at the frontier at the time of settlement, but right up until the 1970s. It also demonstrates the need for, and intrinsic connection between, the oral historian and its subject. Another example of Stolen Generation testimony is evident in Basil Sansom's "In the Absence of Vita as Genre: The Making of the Roy Kelly Story". Sansom worked closely with Kelly to document his life story. Kelly relates to him, as part of Stolen Generations testimony,

> They grabbit baby. Some kid here, he was half caste kid. My little niece that, that half caste baby. You've got one in hospital now. Gubmin will take him. They are going to do it like that agin![38]

This again displays the ability of oral history to give a voice to those who have needed one, to those who have not, and who can not represent themselves. The 1997 *Bringing Them Home* report, which eventually led to an official state apology, was the culmination of Aboriginal testimony regarding the Stolen Generations, testimony which oral historians provided, and concluded in the empowerment of the Aboriginal race.

---

[37] Bain Attwood, "Learning about the Truth: The Stolen Generations narrative", in Bain Attwood and Fiona Magowan, *Telling Stories: Indigenous History and Memory in Australia and New Zealand* (New South Wales, 2001) p.185.
[38] Basil Sansom, "In the Absence of Vita: The Making of the Roy Kelly Story", in Attwood and Magowan, p. 117.

4.5 Righting the wrongs of the past

As mentioned throughout, oral history enables neglected and unrepresented communities to prosper, on their own terms. Often in the cases of Travellers and Aborigines, when they have been represented, they have been misrepresented. The multi-faceted profession of the oral historian then means that they must not only collaborate with members of these communities, but they must try to ascertain the empirical truth, contextualise the findings and finally document and construct history. This has been difficult over the past decades, due to the negativity with which both groups used for this study have been held, both in social and traditional academic terms. The 1990s though witnessed the release of two landmark documents which began to somewhat alter perceptions of both groups. These were the culmination, at the time, of years of endeavour on the part of oral historian's (and other academics of the required fields, such as ethnographers and anthropologists) and both communities' to gain status, ethnicity, and to simply attempt to right some of the wrongs of the past. The *1995 Report of the Task Force on the Travelling Community* and the *1997 Bringing Them Home: National Inquiry into the Separation of Aboriginal and Torres Strait Islander Children from Their Families* were a watershed of sorts in the history of both indigenous groups.

4.5.1 The 1995 Report of the Task Force
on the Travelling Community

In previous paragraphs, the 1963 and 1983 reports regarding Travellers were spoken about. John O' Connell alluded to these as the first and second phase of "a clear and explicit government response to the Travellers of Ireland".[39] For O' Connell, the 1995 was the third phase. It was, arguably, the most important in terms of status and ethnicity of the Travelling community. Unlike previous reports, it devoted a full section to discrimination. The introduction to the discrimination section states,

> The Travelling People Review Body highlighted a range of discrimination experienced by the Travelling community. At the level of individual or interpersonal, it stated: "A local continuing hostility on the part of the settled population in many areas is identified by the Review Body as the greatest factor hindering the provision of accommodation (.....) In recent years a more subtle form of harassment has been practised by certain local

---

[39] O' Connell, p.1.

authorities. This takes the form of fencing off parking areas, even traditional camping sites, or digging trenches around them".[40]

For perhaps the first time in their actual documented history, Travellers were beginning to witness some kind of acknowledgment. There had been no mention of discrimination in previous reports, reports which were incredibly short-sighted and obsolete by the 1990s. As Erica Sheehan asserts, in *Travellers: Citizens of Ireland,* the report represented a "partnership between Travellers and settled people, voluntary organisations, Government Departments and elected representatives."[41] She called it "the most comprehensive examination of the situation of the Travelling community", stating that it "contains significant and convincing proposals for changing the negative issues that Travellers face in Ireland today."[42] Never before had the 'negative issues' facing Travellers been discussed in this form, rather the negative impact of Travellers on Irish society. Therefore, the 1995 report was a veritable turning point, in legislation if nothing else.

The most important aspect of the 1995 report however was the recognition of culture and identity of the Travelling community. The introduction to the culture section of the report states, "Everybody has a culture."[43] Up until that point, Traveller culture was both widely disregarded, and discredited. They were somewhat of a nuisance, and a 'blot' Irish society. It also stated "Traveller nomadism, the importance of the extended family, the Traveller language and the organisation of the Traveller economy all provide visible or tangible markers of a distinct Traveller culture."[44] Helleiner points out that, unlike previous reports, "The labels of both 'Traveller' and 'Settled' were consistently capitalised, and a model of 'interculturalism' was used to describe relations between Travellers and non-Traveller communities".[45] Therefore, as often and in as many ways as possible, the culture and status of the community was recognised. The conclusion of the culture section of the report states, "Nobody's culture can be destroyed, wiped out or assimilated."[46] This statement is particularly at odds with previous government policies of

---

[40] *1995 Report of the Task Force on the Travelling Community,* (Dublin, 1995) p.78.
[41] Sheehan, p.215.
[42] Ibid.
[43] *1995 Report of the Task Force on the Travelling Community,* p.71.
[44] Ibid, p.72.
[45] Helleiner, p.236.
[46] *1995 Report of the Task Force on the Travelling Community,* p.76.

assimilation and settlement, without consultation or representation. The key statement, arguably, in the whole report is the 'Recommendation' of the culture section, which reads, "That the distinct culture and identity of the Travelling community be recognised and taken into account."[47] This statement is perhaps the very essence of this study; the quest for history, status and recognition and representation, and the amount of time and hardship taken with which to earn it. There are still, quite clearly, debates regarding the ethnic status of the community, both in academic and social circles. Many still refute Traveller claims to ethnicity. Former Irish Minister for Justice, Michael McDowell, for example, has argued against the ethnic status of the community. For practitioners in the field, Travellers are indeed an ethnic group, and oral historians have endeavoured more than most to entrench this. Oral testimony has consequently been vital not only in the construction of history, but in the pursuit of ethnicity.

Aboriginal Man hunting with a spear[48]

---

[47] Ibid.

[48] Sincere gratitude is extended to: http://news.softpedia.com/newsImage/Who-Are-the-Australian-Aborigines-2.jpg/ - for their kindness in permitting us to use this image: (Accessed: 10/12/2010).

The 1995 report was therefore a landmark document in the history of Irish Travellers. After decades, perhaps even centuries, of discrimination, neglect and misrepresentation, the Travelling community were finally recognised as that which they had always considered themselves to be; a distinct and separate ethnic group. Without the testimony gathered, contextualised and structured by oral historians the construction of Irish Traveller history and the subsequent notion of ethnicity would not have been, and indeed would not continue to be possible. Oral history has then been vital in the empowerment of the Travelling community.

4.5.2 The 1997 'Bringing Them Home' report

The 1997 *Bringing Them Home: National Inquiry into the Separation of Aboriginal and Torres Strait Islander Children from Their Families* is comparative in many ways to the *Report of the Task Force on the Travelling Community* two years previous. It was also the culmination of decades, and again, probably centuries, of oppression and marginalisation. The report was a direct consequence of the aforementioned Stolen Generations. The merits of oral history and testimony can be witnessed here, as the report was constructed in terms of testimony from those 'stolen' Aborigines. The report commission was established in 1995, by the former Australian Attorney-General, Michael Lavarch, in response to,

> Increasing concern among key indigenous agencies and communities that the general public's ignorance of the history of forcible removal was hindering the recognition of the needs of its victims and their families and the provision of services.[49]

Such was the traumatic nature relating the events of the Stolen Generations for the witnesses, personal and psychological support was needed during and after. Psychologist, Dr. Jane McKendrick states, in the report, "I know a lot of people who have become extremely distraught at the thought of this inquiry, because a lot of people psychologically have put that- a lot of what happened- to the back of their minds."[50] A section of the report is even titled "Services for those Affected". The task for the oral historian was therefore much greater, as there was not simply a straight-forward relating and re-telling of events. The Inquiry took evidence orally, or in

---

[49] *Bringing Them Home: National Inquiry into the Separation of Aboriginal and Torres Strait Islander Children from Their Families,* (New South Wales, 1997) p.18.
[50] Ibid, p.19.

writing from 535 indigenous people concerning their experiences of the removal policies.[51] The report itself relays many of these. When put into context, this encompasses a very small percentage of the estimated near 100,000 who were 'stolen'. The notion of the 'voice for the voiceless', and the empowerment of the indigenous races through oral testimony are vividly evident in the pages of the report. Examples of the trauma, yet representation, include,

> Most of us girls were thinking white in the head but were feeling black inside. We weren't black inside. We were a lonely, lost and sad displaced people. We were taught to think and act like a white person, but we didn't know how to think and act like an Aboriginal. We didn't know anything about our culture.[52]

Indigenous Deaths in Custody Banner[53]

---

[51] Ibid, p.21.

[52] Ibid, p.152.

[53] Sincere thanks is extended to: http://www.indybay.org/newsitems/2009/04/04/18586071.php for their kindness in permitting us to use this image: (Accessed: 10/12/2010).

Another Aboriginal girl, in the Western Australia section of the inquiry, describes,

> When I was about twelve or thirteen years old I was taken to Moola Bulla. That's where I lost my Aboriginal ways. The Police came down one day (...) and found me, a half-caste child. The manager told my people, my mum and dad, that they were taking me to Fitzroy Crossing for a trip. They did not know that I would never see them again.[54]

This was particularly horrific in relation to the cases of thousands of Aboriginal children and their families. The girl who gave this testimony was, as it says, twelve of thirteen, meaning she already knew about her culture and values, and was being taken to remove her of these. This was the sad reality for the Aboriginal race for much of the twentieth century.

For Rosanne Kennedy, the distinction must be made between oral history narratives and symbolic narratives, which she separates as chronicle and interpretation.[55] This places the oral historian in an awkward position of power, particularly with regard to the Stolen Generations, and the Bringing Them home report. The historian must chronicle yet construct and interpret traumatic events, and in this case it was for the empowerment of the Aboriginal race, and the righting of the atrocities of the Australian past. Kennedy asserts that the testimony "does not ask for our empathy"[56], rather it serves to correct the 'denial' of Aboriginal history, to construct and document that which has not previously been represented in the annals of history.

As she goes on to point out, "it asks White Australians to work out where we fit into this history of separation, and into Aboriginal history more broadly".[57] In this way, the Bringing Them Home report is an inquiry in racism and racist practices, which the indigenous people of Australia had been subjected to for over two hundred years. The report then must be quantified as a landmark document, perhaps *the* landmark document in Aboriginal history. The *Bringing Them Home* report was the most significant in a line of events concerning the 'righting of the wrongs' of the past in the 1990s. Others included the various acquisitions of land rights, native title and status of the race. The report, while not quite, almost qualified as an apology, as it was a government-led inquiry into crimes which had been committed, despite the fact that, at the time, they had been government policy. The apology would not materialise until over

---

[54] Ibid, p.107.
[55] Kennedy, in Perks and Thomson, p.516
[56] Ibid, p.518
[57] Ibid.

Image of Eddie Mabo's headstone – Eddie Mabo was one of the first Aboriginal civil rights activists.[58]

a decade later. Prime Minister at the time of the report, John Howard, rejected calls for an official apology. His government's response was "that these administrators thought they were acting in the best interests of the children"[59], to which Robert Manne rejoined "the Nazis also had good intentions."[60] As Macintyre attains, *"Bringing Them Home* called for reparation to the victims of child removal by monetary compensation and other means", but above all, arguably for the Aboriginal race at least, "it sought apologies from the governments, churches and other agencies that had created the Stolen Generations."[61] As mentioned, Howard would not agree to an official government apology, as "such a step would be to admit

---

[58] Sincere thanks is extended to: http://www.nfsa.gov.au/digitallearning/mabo/info/ eMTombstoneOpening.htm for their kindness in permitting us to use this image: (Accessed: 10/12/2010).

[59] Macintyre, *The History Wars,* p.145.

[60] Ibid.

[61] Ibid, p.154.

liability and open the way to financial claims, and that no government could be expected to apologise for the actions of a predecessor."[62] This statement would appear to be incredibly short-sighted in terms of national apologies made by leading statesmen and women, such as Tony Blair and Angela Merkel, in recent years.

Pope Benedict the Sixteenth chats with an Aboriginal man while on a visit to Australia[63]

The Australian apology finally came on the 13th of February, 2008 from Australian premier, Kevin Rudd, over a decade after the inquiry that proposed it. Rudd began his speech, in parliament that morning at 9.30am, by saying 'sorry' three times for the victims of the official government policy that was the Stolen Generations,

"As Prime Minister of Australia, I am sorry. On behalf of the government of Australia, I am sorry. On behalf of the parliament of Australia, I am sorry. I offer you this apology without qualification".[64]

---

[62] Ibid, p.155.
[63] Sincere thanks is extended to: http://www.sbs.com.au/news/resize/index/id/ 39372/w/450/h/338/jpeg/81960012abomain_1216367783.jpg for their kindness in permitting us to use this image: (Accessed: 10/12/2010).
[64] Kevin Rudd, "Full text of Kevin Rudd's speech", *Herald Sun*, 13 February 2008

Kevin Rudd, PM Australia 2007 to June 2010. The First Australian Prime Minister to issue an apology to the "Stolen Generations".[65]

John Howard did not attend the apology, stating, "I will not be in Canberra next week".[66]

Oral history and historian can certainly take a large amount of credit for the apology offered to the Aboriginal people by the Australian government. Their work has allowed the Aboriginal people, like the Travellers of Ireland, to enter the historical construct, which led to the 1997 *Bringing them Home* report. This report paved the way for the inevitable Australian official apology, and has empowered a previously unrepresented and neglected people.

---

[65] Sincere gratitude is extended to: http://www.australianclimatemadness.com/ ?tag=kevin-rudd - for their kindness in permitting us to use this image: (Accessed: 10/12/2010).

[66] Adam Gartrell, "Howard will not attend apology", *The Sydney Morning Herald,* 8 February 2008.

CHAPTER FIVE

CONCLUSION:
POSTCOLONIAL HISTORIES

Aboriginal Male launching a decorated boomerang[1]

---

[1] Sincere thanks is extended to: http://news.softpedia.com/newsImage/Who-Are-the-Australian-Aborigines-3.jpeg/ - for their kindness in permitting us to use this image: (Accessed: 10/12/2010).

Eddie Mabo – Aboriginal Rights Activist[2]

---

[2] Sincere thanks is extended to: http://www.hsc.csu.edu.au/ab_studies/rights/
global/social_justice_global/sjwelcome.response.front.htm - for their kindness in
permitting us to use this image: (Accessed: 10/12/2010).

5.1 Conclusion

Irish Travellers and Australian Aborigines are, and always will be, the indigenous peoples of their respective countries. They will always have been undocumented and unrepresented in the past. In the present, however, these two neglected social groups have entered the realm of documented history, and have become represented and empowered. In this regard, the future may lead to a representation of their own making. Oral history has given power to these groups, a 'voice to the voiceless'. It has reconstructed their lives, both in the past and present. It has also have provided them with the ability to construct and represent themselves in the future.

This volume has attempted to assess the contribution of oral history in the construction, representation and, in turn, empowerment of Irish Travellers and Australian Aborigines. A key factor that was learned during the course of the project was that all three aspects of the study, oral history, the history of Irish Travellers and the history of Australian Aborigines, are all relatively new departments in academic history. Comparatively, all three became somewhat popular in the 1950s and 1960s. As oral history became more popular in the postcolonial era, so too did the history of Othering and history from below. These new historical factions were not viewed positively by traditional, establishment historians, and thus began life in historical discourse at a disadvantage. Considering neglected social groups needed oral history for representation, they were considered almost 'non-historical' in traditional terms, due the lack of a linear or documented history.

While these groups had the lack of support from traditional historians to contend with, they were then faced with the problem of truth and objectivity regarding oral testimony. Oral testimony, particularly that of groups without a documented history, can be extremely contentious; a fact which has been at the epicentre of the Australian 'History Wars', and has created problems for the history of the Travelling community. Therefore, oral historians must, and have arguably succeeded in relation to these groups, contextualise all their findings in objective a manner as possible. In the future, it may be possible for members of the groups themselves to carry out this objective contextualisation.

Histories of postcolonial nations, at least "traditional" histories, are written in favour of the coloniser. Therefore, in the case of both groups used in this study, attempt at documenting and representing them are skewed from the outset; firstly by the fact they are indigenous to postcolonial countries, and secondly, due to their marginalisation within those countries. It is therefore testament to oral history that the representation and empowerment of these groups has occurred, despite problems such as cultural legitimacy, Othering, ethnocentrism and the obvious lack of chronicled history.

This volume has thus endeavoured to prove the intrinsic role played by oral history in the history of neglected social groups. It also set out to examine why oral history has been so important to the past, present and future of Irish Travellers and Australian Aborigines, in terms of what is already known, i.e. what little documented history that has been produced over the past century. Oral testimony, as mentioned, is vital to groups who lack the ability, or even propensity to create their own construct of their past. The chronicled past, for them, has been one that is the subject of debate for historical scholars, rather than one that has been the subject of enquiry from those same scholars. Oral history has helped to alter this scenario in recent decades.

Aborginal Cave Art[3]

Government policy regarding Travellers and Aborigines was also a significant aspect of this study. This policy is particularly relevant for two reasons; firstly, most government policy up until the end the twentieth century, involving both groups was carried out without consultation or input from either group, and secondly, oral testimony was needed to attempt to rectify these policies in the latter days of the century. The Stolen Generations and the *1963 Report of the Commission on Itinerancy* were the examples used to demonstrate the attempted forced assimilation

---

[3] Sincere gratitude is extended to: http://news.softpedia.com/newsImage/Who-Are-the-Australian-Aborigines-4.jpg/- for their kindness in permitting us to use this image: (Accessed: 10/12/2010).

of both groups into mainstream society. Such was the horrific nature of the Stolen Generations that Australian Prime Minister, Kevin Rudd made a public apology in parliament in 2008, which had been alluded to in the landmark *Bringing Them Home* report in 1997. For Irish Travellers, there was no apology. There was, however, the recognition of ethnic status in 1995, as a result of the 1995 *Report of the Task Force on the Travelling Community.*

As we move forward in the second decade of the twenty-first century, things are slowly beginning to change for neglected social groups such as Irish Travellers and Australian Aborigines. The close comparisons between them mean that collaboration of scholars of both groups in the future could lead to the further empowerment regarding both history and social status. Negative stereotypes still overwhelmingly exist towards both groups in their homelands. However, as oral history and testimony has provided a past, it has also provided a platform and a social confidence which will arguably enable members of both groups to better themselves, and in the future perhaps a historical and social construct of their own making. Oral history has therefore attributed greatly to the social and historical empowerment of both Irish Travellers and Australian Aborigines.

REFERENCES

The Irish Folklore Commission 1952 Tinker Questionnaire (Dublin, 1952)

1963 Report of the Commission on Itinerancy (Dublin, 1963)

1983 Report of the Travelling People Review Board (Dublin, 1983)

1995 Report of the Task Force on the Travelling Community (Dublin, 1995)

1995 Report of the Task Force on the Travelling Community: Executive Summary, (Dublin, 1995)

"Aboriginal" testimony in Attwood, Bain and Magowan, Fiona (eds.), *Telling Stories: Indigenous History in Australia and New Zealand* (New South Wales, 2001)

Bringing Them Home: National Inquiry into the Separation of Aboriginal and Torres Strait Islander Children from Their Families, April 1997 (New South Wales, 1997)

Joyce, Nan and Farmar, Anna (ed.), *My Life on the Road: An Autobiography by Nan Joyce* (Dublin, 2000)

Letter transcripts, in Henry Reynolds, *Dispossession: Black Australians and White Invaders* (New South Wales, 1989)

Abrams, Donald, Hogg, Michael and Marques, José (eds.), *The Social Psychology of Inclusion and* Exclusion (New York, 2005)

Acton, Thomas and Hayes, Michael (eds.), *Counter-Hegemony and the Post-Colonial "Other"* (Newcastle, 2006)

Atkinson, Paul and Hammersley, Martin, *Ethnography: Principles in Practice (3rd Ed.)* (New York, 2007)

Attwood, Bain, *Telling the Truth about Aboriginal History,* (New South Wales, 2005)

Attwood, Bain and MacGowan, Fiona (eds.), *Telling Stories: Indigenous History and Memory in Australia and New Zealand* (New South Wales, 2001)

Beams, Nick, "What is at stake in Australia's History Wars?", at *World Socialist Web Site,* 16 July 2004.

Benjamin, Andrew et al. (eds.) (2002) *Postcolonial Cultures and Literatures: Modernity and the (Un)commonwealth*: New York: Peter Lang

Bhreatnach, Aoife, *Becoming Conspicuous: Irish Travellers, Society and State 1922-1970* (Dublin, 2006)

Bolton, Geoffrey, *The Oxford History of Australia: Volume 5 The Middle Way 1942-1995* (Melbourne, 1996)

Broussard, J.C. *Giving a Voice to the Voiceless: Four Pioneering Black Women Journalists;* (New York, 2003)

Burke, Peter (ed.), *History and Historians in the Twentieth Century* (New York, 2002)

—. (ed.), *New Perspectives on Historical Writing (2nd Ed.)* (Oxford, 2002)

Borland, Katherine, "'That's not what I said' Interpretative Conflict in Oral Narrative Research", in

Charlton, T.L.., Myers, L.E. and Sharpless, Rebecca (eds.), *Handbook of Oral History* (Plymouth, 2006)

Comaroff, John and Jean, *Ethnography and the Historical Imagination* (Oxford, 1992)

Court, A. (1985) *Puck of the Droms: the lives and literature of the Irish tinkers*. California: University of California Press

Crowley, Niall, "Travellers", in McCormack, W.J., *The Blackwell Companion to Modern Irish Culture* (Oxford, 1999)

Denzin, Norman K., *Interpretive Ethnography: Ethnographic Practices in the 21st Century* (London, 1997)

Dillon, Eamon, *The Outsiders: Exposing the Secretive World of Ireland's Travellers* (Dublin 2006)

Eagleton, T. (1991) *Ideology*; London: Verso

Ezzaher, Lahcen E., *Writing and Cultural Influence* (Oxford, 2003)

Fanon, Frantz, *Black Skin, White Masks* (London, 1967)

—. *The Wretched of the Earth* (London, 1963)

Feldstein, Martin, "Kissing Cousins: Journalism and Oral History", in *Oral History Review* (2004)

Ferriter, Diarmuid, *The Transformation of Ireland 1900-2000* (London, 2004)

Fox-Genovese, Elizabeth and Lasch-Quinn, Elisabeth, *Reconstructing History: The Emergence of a New Historical Society* (New York, 1999)

Gartrell, Adam, "Howard will not attend apology", *The Sydney Morning Herald,* 8 February 2008

Gmelch, George, *The Irish Tinkers: The Urbanisation of an Itinerant People* (Illinois, 1985)

—. "The Emergence of an Ethnic Group: Irish Tinkers", in *Anthropological Quarterly* (1976)

—. *Tinkers and Travellers: Ireland's Nomads* (Dublin, 1975)

Hall, Catherine, "Histories, Empires and the Post-Colonial Moment", in Chambers, Iain And Curti, Lidia, *The Post-Colonial Question: Common Skies, Divided Horizons* (London, 1996)

Hamilton, Paula and Shopes Linda (eds.), *Oral History and Public Memories* (Philadelphia, 2008)

Hamilton, Paula, "The Oral Historian as Memorist", in *Oral History Review* (2005)

Hammond, Ross A. and Axelrod, Robert, "The Evolution of Ethnocentrism", in *Journal of Conflict Resolution, Vol.50.* (2006)

Hartley, John and McKee, Alan, *The Indigenous Public Sphere: The Reporting and Reception of Indigenous Issues in the Australian Media, 1994-1997* (New York, 2000)

Healy, T. (1992) New Latitudes : Theory and English Renaissance Literature; London: Edward Arnold

Helleiner, Jane, *Irish Travellers: Racism and the Politics of Culture* (Toronto, 2000

Hirsh, Jerrold, "Before Columbia: The FWP and American Oral History Research", in *Oral History Review* (2007)

Hodgkin, Kathleen And Radstone, Susanne (eds.), *Contested Pasts: The Politics of Memory* (New York, 2003)

Howarth, Ken, *Oral History: A Handbook* (Glouchestershire, 1998)

Jones, Tony, "Authors in History Debate: Macintyre and Windschuttle", on *Lateline,* Australian Broadcasting Corporation, 3 September 2003.

Jordanova, Ludmilla, *History in Practice (2nd Ed.)* (New York, 2006)

Keating, Paul, "Reflections on the History Wars: The political battle for Australia's future", at *Online Opinion,* 12 September 2003.

Kennedy, Rosanne, "Stolen Generation Testimony: Trauma, Historiography and the Question of 'Truth'", in Perks, Robert and Thomson, Alistair (eds.), *The Oral History Reader (2nd Ed.)* (London, 2006)

Kenrick, Donald, "The Travellers of Ireland", in *The Patrin Web Journal* (1998)

Gupta, C. and Chattopadhyaya D. P., *Cultural Otherness and Beyond,* (Leiden, 1998)

Kearney, R., *Strangers, Gods and Monsters: Interpreting Otherness,* (London, 2002)

Kirby, R.K., "Phenomenology and the Problems of Oral History", in *Oral History Review* (2008)

Lanters, J. (2008) *The 'Tinkers' in Irish Literature.* Dublin: Irish Academic Press

Lentin, Ronit and McVeigh, Robbie, *After Optimism? Ireland, Racism and Globalisation* (Dublin, 2006)

Lummins, Trevor, "Structure and Validity in Oral Evidence", in Perks, Robert and Thomson, Alistair (eds.), *The Oral History Reader* (New York, 2006)

Macintyre, Stuart, *A Concise History of Australia,* (Melbourne, 2004)

—. *The History Wars,* (Melbourne, 2003)

MacLaughlin, Jim, *Travellers and Ireland: Whose Country, Whose History?* (Cork, 1995)

Marx, Karl, *The Eighteenth Brumaire of Louis Napoleon* (Moscow, 1954)

McCormick, A. (1907) *The Tinkler Gypsies*; Dumfries, Scotland: Maxwell

McDonagh, Martin, "Origins of the Travelling People", in Sheehan, E. (ed.), *Travellers: Citizens of Ireland* (Dublin, 2000)

Melleuish, Greg, "Leave History Alone", *The Australian,* 1 September 2009

McGrath, Ann (ed.), *Contested Ground: Australian Aborigines under the British Crown* (New South Wales, 1995)

Meadows, Michael, *Voices in the Wilderness: Images of Aboriginal People in the Australian Media* (Connecticut, 2001)

Moran A. "The Psychodynamics of Australian Settler-Nationalism: Assimilating or Reconciling with the Aborigines?" in *International Society of Political Psychology*, Vol. 23, No. 4 (Dec., 2002)

Nile, Richard, *Australian Aborigines* (Illinois, 1993)

Nkwi, W.G., Voicing the Voiceless. Contributions to Closing Gaps in Cameroon History, 1958-2009   (Michigan, 2010)

Nugent, Maria, "Mapping Memories", in Hamilton, Paula and Shopes, Linda (eds.), *Oral History and Public Memories* (Philadelphia, 2008)

O' Connell, John, "Travellers in Ireland: An Examination of Discrimination and Racism", *Pavee Point Travellers Centre,* January 1998

Ó hAodha, Mícheál (ed.), *Migrants and Memory: The Forgotten Postcolonials* (Newcastle, 2007)

Partington, Geoffrey, *The Australian History of Henry Reynolds,* (Adelaide, 2004)

Patel, Niti Sampat , *Postcolonial Masquerades: Culture and Politics in Literature, Film, Video, and Photography* (New York, 2001)

Perks, Robert and Thompson, Alistair (eds.), *The Oral History Reader* (London, 1998)

Perks, Robert and Thompson, Alistair (eds.), *The Oral History Reader (2ⁿᵈ Ed.)* (London, 2006)

Povinelli, Elizabeth A. (2002) *The Cunning of Recognition: Indigenous Alterities and the making of Australian Multiculturalism*; Durham [N.C.]: Duke University Press

Portelli, Alessandro, *The Death of Luigi Trastulli and Other Stories: Form and Meaning in Oral History* (New York, 1991)

—. *The Order Has Been Carried Out: History, Memory and Meaning of a Nazi Massacre in Rome* (New York, 2003)

Prentis, Malcolm, *A Study in Black and White: The Aborigines in Australian History* (Sydney, 1975)

Reynolds, Henry, *Dispossession: Black Australians and White Invaders* (New South Wales, 1989)

—. *Frontier: Reports from the Edge of White Settlement* (New South Wales, 1987)

Richardson, Darlene, "Reconstructing a Community with Oral History", in *Oral History Review* (2002)

Ritchie, Donald P., *Doing Oral History* (New York, 1995)

—. *Doing Oral History (2nd Ed.)* (New York, 2003)

Rudd, Kevin, "Full text of Kevin Rudd's speech", *Herald Sun*, 13 February 2008

Said, E. (1993) *Culture and Imperialism*; London: Chatto and Windus

Said, Edward, *Orientalism: Western Conceptions of the Orient* (London, 1978)

Scates, B. (1997) *A New Australia: Citizenship, Radicalism and the First Republic;* Cambridge: Cambridge University Press

Sansom, Basil, "In the Absence of Vita: The Making of the Roy Kelly story", in Attwood, Bain and Magowan, Fiona (eds.), *Telling Stories: Indigenous History and Memory in Australia and New Zealand* (New South Wales, 2001)

Sharpe, Jim, "History from Below", in Burke, P. (ed.), *New Perspectives on Historical Writing (2nd Ed.)* (Oxford, 2002)

Sharpless Rebecca, "The History of Oral History", in Charlton et al, *Handbook of Oral History* (Plymouth, 2006)

Sheehan, Erica (ed.), *Travellers: Citizens of Ireland* (Dublin, 2000)

Taylor, Penny, *Telling it like it is: A Guide to Making Aboriginal and Torres Strait Islander History* (Canberra, 1992)

Thomson, Alistair, "Four Paradigm Transformations in Oral History", in *Oral History Review* (2006)

Thompson, Paul, *The Voice of the Past* (Oxford, 1978)

Tonkin, Elizabeth, *Narrating Our Pasts: The Social Construction of Oral History* (Cambridge, 1992)

Tosh, John, *The Pursuit of History (4th Ed.)* (Harlow, UK, 2006)

Walsh, Christine and Ó hAodha, Míchael (ed.), *Postcolonial Borderlands: Orality and Irish Traveller Writing* (Newcastle, 2008)

76 References

Welsh, Frank, *Great Southern Land: A New History of Australia* (London, 2004)

Windschuttle, Keith, *The Fabrication of Aboriginal History* (Sydney, 2002)